COUNTRY STYLE
‑ AUSTRALIA ‑

COUNTRY STYLE
- AUSTRALIA -

Beryl Clarke Marchi
& Ray Jarratt

For Roz on Christmas '91
To provide good memories of
OZ wherever we may roam
XO, Andy

To Roz
Merry Christmas '91
We hope you enjoy
reading this book
Love Kelly

To Ros
merry Christmas
Love Andrew

RANDOM HOUSE
AUSTRALIA

PAGE 1
*In the bay window of an old house a
soft light illuminates a faience bowl
and flowers in a jug.*

PAGE 2
*The charming living room of a
Georgian house on the Shoalhaven
River displays an Arthur Boyd canvas.*

RIGHT
*A tangle of vines grows over the french
doors of a Blue Mountains house built
of weatherboard.*

Random House Australia
an imprint of
Random Century Australia Pty Ltd
20 Alfred Street, Milsons Point NSW 2061
Sydney Melbourne London
Auckland Johannesburg
and agencies throughout the world

Created and designed by Barbara Beckett Publishing
14 Hargrave St. Paddington, Australia 2021

First published 1991

Text copyright © Beryl Clarke Marchi
Photographs copyright © Ray Jarratt

National Library of Australia
Cataloguing-in-Publication Data
Clarke Marchi, Beryl
    Country style Australia
    ISBN 0 09 182601 2.
    1. Interior decoration—Australia.   2.
    Decoration and ornament, Rustic—
    Australia.   I. Jarratt, Ray.   II. Title
747.2994
Printed in Hong Kong
Production by Vantage Graphics, Sydney

ACKNOWLEDGEMENTS

TO ALL the people whose enthusiasm for our project made them offer so much help, a heartfelt thank-you. First, for their generous offering of an open house at Bundanon, we are deeply indebted to Arthur Boyd and his wife, Yvonne. David and Clarissa Mort we cannot thank enough for their unstinting help and hospitality. To Jock Mort, a special thank-you for his blithe presence. For sharing that good country feeling, we thank Sheila Carroll for making us welcome and helping us so mightily. Carol Orford was kind and understanding and always generous with her time. To Emma Schofield, our sincere thanks for being such a trusting aid to our project.

Sue Curtis has our warmest thanks and admiration for taking such pains and being so generous with her time. To Wendy Kelly thanks for such help and hospitality. To Dawn Town and Roz Muir-Smith, thanks for aiding and abetting us with unstinting hospitality and friendship. Ruth Turnell gave her time generously and we appreciated her support and understanding. To Maria Prendergast, a champion in every way, our sincere and lasting thanks.

To Michael Pritchard and Dean Kempnick our thanks for so much help and generous hospitality. We thank Lyndsay Pratt for taking time to help us so willingly when there were other pressing things on his mind. For a job so beautifully done we offer Evelyn Bloom both congratulations and thanks for her enthusiastic co-operation.

Trish Hurst deserves a very special thank-you, not only for helping us so generously with advice and information, but because her enthusiasm for the subject of 'country' never falters for a moment.

To John Williams, Glenn Murcutt and Max Dupain, our cordial thanks for their very professional co-operation.

Peter Watts, Director of the Historic Houses Trust of New South Wales, and Sue Hunt, Senior Curator Houses, have our sincere thanks for their help, concern and interest. We also thank Elaine Lawson, Curator of Lanyon, ACT, for such efficient and caring help to us.

For those photographs not taken by Ray Jarratt, our thanks are due to the following photographers: Max Dupain, pp. 20, 21, 130, 131, 132, 133, 134, 135; Ray Joyce, pp. 6, 12, 13, 14, 15, 18, 19, 30, 31, 44, 45, 60, 61; Neil Lorrimer, pp. 11, 35, 94, 95, 96, 97, 98, 99, 100, 101, 102, 103, 122, 123, 238, 241, 242; and Richard Woldendorp, p. 17.

For permission to reproduce photographs of the following items, we would like to thank the National Library of Australia for the embroidered bag on p. 230; the New South Wales Department of Education for the children's dresses on pp. 230 and 231; the Embroiderers' Guild for the embroidered wattle on p. 232; and the Museum of Applied Arts and Sciences (now the Powerhouse Museum) for the engraved glass and silver gilt enamelled box and pencil case on p. 235.

*This old Queensland house has all the
familiar earmarks of its genre; lattice
is used to advantage for climate
control.*

CONTENTS

WHAT IS COUNTRY STYLE?

WHEN I told a friend in London that I was working on this book, she was puzzled. 'But what *is* Australian country style?' she asked. I painted her a word picture. It was an interesting exercise. For those who recognise Australian country style as an idiomatic thing, it comes as a surprise to have to define it. Still, definitions are always helpful, so let's attempt to categorise it. Primarily Australian country style is an unpretentious approach to making a house into a home. It unselfconsciously rates people above possessions, comfort before contrivance, and practicality above all. The word *uncomplicated* best describes it.

Country style is not concerned with interior decoration

Reflections in a lake, Ilford, New South Wales

Rural peace and tranquil water, Mudgee, New South Wales

per se. Its real involvement is with the making of a home. At its most natural it's a collection of things acquired and used through several generations of family life. But today such family things are rarities. Because succeeding generations have been caught up with the passing fancies of fashion, few of us possess handed-down treasures to furnish our homes. The past few decades have shown such decisive decorating trends, from Scandinavian style to Post-Modern, that many of us have been mesmerised into following the fads. But during those decades simple country style has gone its own comfortable way, remaining true to certain intrinsic values.

The values of good craftsmanship in furniture making,

Standing like tall sentinels beside this charming old farmhouse in Victoria, these water tanks provide a generous water supply.

*On either side of a dusty South
Australian road, grapevines grow
lushly in season. Beyond, the old
farmhouse can be seen.*

the simplicity of hand-woven textiles and handmade ceramics, the genuine enthusiasm for honest craft in all its
forms—all these are embodied in the old-fashioned ethic
of country simplicity and honesty. Country style has much
to do with items of virtue. If they carry the scars of age
it's no detriment. Old, well-loved things that show their
ancestry and their time-worn utility have a distinctive
quality that endears them to us. And because they have
touched the lives of others, they have great value for us
today as a link with the past.

Rooms with self-conscious style, with carefully co-
ordinated schemes, decorated with shiny new accessories,
are at the farthest remove from country style. But rooms
that say 'lived-in' say country style; rooms with a cosy

*In the golden afternoon light, this
Ipswich house has the mellow character
of an old family home, with all its
remembered comforts.*

OPPOSITE PAGE
*A fine symmetry of line can be seen in
the classic Queensland design of this
old house. The arches in the lattice
screen are very fine.*

WHAT IS COUNTRY STYLE?

Near Maryborough, this weathered
building has lost none of its charm,
although its painted surfaces are
peeling and the corrugated-iron roof is
rusted.

clutter of baskets, books, family photographs and bric-à-brac say it best. Of course, the clutter must have a certain orderliness; the dead-flowers-and-dust school of decorating has no place here. The most appealing aspect of country style is that it's relaxed and it's comfortable; but above all else, it's lived-in.

People with a natural bowerbird instinct are enthusiastic adherents to the look of country style. Let's say you find a beaten-up old wicker whatnot in a second-hand store in some country town. If you know at first glance that it would look shabby and out of place in your living room, forget it. But if you can take it home, fill it with half a dozen potted primulas in bloom and find it fits in as if made for the place, then you're probably already on the threshold of living in country style.

It seems that something singular has happened to us in

Standing high on its stilts, this typical Queensland house makes an unusual patch of blue in an otherwise green landscape.

recent years. We've begun setting our sights on a very different kind of lifestyle. With the growing awareness of our planet's degradation, we have become more concerned with the verity of things close to home. The cult of consumerism is being questioned: we are aware that our homes can hold only so many 'things'. We have begun asking ourselves just exactly what it is we want in our homes. And the answer is that we want simplicity, comfort and harmony. With a fresh view of the true values in life, we have begun to appreciate the wonderful ease and aesthetic rewards of Australian country style. We're experiencing a brand new love of country.

Elizabeth Farm, Parramatta, New South Wales

Robert Juniper's unique house,
Western Australia

OPPOSITE PAGE
Beside the bleached and weathered walls
on this old veranda, a couple of beds
testify to the need for sleeping cool.

ABOVE
A typical lived-in space, this veranda
is the prototype of all such Australian
outdoor-indoor comfort zones.

ABOVE
Inside, the vibrant colour of huge paintings seems like an extension of the surrounding terrain, which is natural rock-strewn bush.

OPPOSITE PAGE
This striking house was designed by Glenn Murcutt for the artist Sidney Ball. The interior space is brilliantly conceived.

A corner of the living room at
Bundanon, Shoalhaven

At the entrance of Little Tallawangra,
Mudgee, New South Wales

'We are looking back to softer, homier times, choosing the beauty of
natural materials and enjoying the thrill of finding worthy old objects'

WHAT IS COUNTRY STYLE?

*The living room of Rebecca
Chapman's small cottage. Rebecca
made the curtains and cushions and
wallpapered the room herself.*

*One of the two charming garden rooms
at Elizabeth Farm*

WHAT IS COUNTRY STYLE?

Morning tea under the honeysuckle at Rebecca Chapman's house, served on a hand-embroidered cloth. The tea cosy was hand-knitted, and the crocheted cover on the milk jug is beaded to weigh down the edge.

The back veranda of the Chapman cottage. In the background is a Huon pine dresser; at the right, a primitive Australian pine hall cupboard.

'Old, well-loved things that show their ancestry and their time-worn utility have a distinctive quality that endears them to us'

CREATING THE COUNTRY LOOK

The Tunbridge ware tea caddy, made of veneered and inlaid hardwoods, is dated circa 1820; around it a small collection of berry spoons and china. Such burgeoning collections are at the very heart of country style.

IF the relaxed and comfortable look of country style is what you want for your house, you'll find it is surprisingly easy to achieve. And as the country look is very much in tune with environmental awareness, it's appropriate for this day and age.

The fact that it can be acquired in easy stages is a further point in its favour. Perhaps your first step should be to take a look in any attic or storeroom or garage where family things might have come to rest over the years. If you're lucky, you could be rewarded for your efforts at the outset. You may be surprised to find that certain long-forgotten objects, when salvaged, look interesting to you for the first time. Don't be surprised if polishing up some old brass drawer handles, knitting a few replacement squares for Grandmother's afghan coverlet, or sanding back the splinters on an ancient chair seem like fascinating projects. Now that you've heard the Pied Piper's tune, you'll be an eager traveller on the country road.

Let us imagine that you have become a true and dedicated enthusiast. What will the next step be? If it happens that you are just beginning your home decorating, it should be very easy; you can take a purist's approach. But otherwise you'll need to begin subtracting a few objects that have begun to seem out of place. The chrome or glass that kept you polishing in the past can now be relegated to the attic, storeroom or garage; sleek, hi-tech, modern things have little relevance in the country scene.

A white picket fence seems to emphasise the rather more intricate form of the lattice adorning the veranda's shady area.

WHEN you set out to create the country look you'll be taking a step toward a much more relaxed way of life. Your home will seem more easy and comfortable. Even more enticing is the anticipation of years of satisfaction ahead as you search for ever better and more interesting examples of the country genre. The bonus will be your widening knowledge; the history and provenance of each item you find will bring to life the story of our past, not the big sweeping events of history but the simple domestic tales that are so heart-warming.

So where do you begin this change of scene? First, let's consider floors. Bare boards with rugs are *de rigueur*. But what if your floors aren't in presentable condition? Then coir matting is inexpensive and next to the best thing. Its natural tone is the ideal base for almost any colour scheme you may devise. Next, the walls; bagged brick, painted brick, or plain white never fails. To disguise impossibly bumpy walls, wallpapers in small, busy floral prints may be used; rich deep colour tones in paint can be handsome, but they don't disguise unevenness. Wooden

*This double-decker veranda has
wonderfully ornate architectural detail
in the arches and fretwork that gives it
such style.*

A fresh looking bedroom in yellow. Rebecca Chapman made the curtains and bedcover as well as wallpapering this room in her country house.

CREATING THE COUNTRY LOOK

The second bedroom in Rebecca Chapman's house, with a fine old bedcover rescued from an op-shop. The simple bedside table is actually a stool covered with three layers of fabric and topped with glass.

Seen from the bedroom, the bare linoleum floor and vertically laid lining boards for the painted walls are typical of many country houses.

Old pine pieces, a mesh-sided pantry safe and a simple dresser, get a touch of festivity from the big basket of dried flowers in the centre of the room where a mellow old carpet lies.

The faded paint and delicate treillage of an old aviary makes a pretty vista from the windows of a rather austere dining room.

panelling, wainscoting and chair rails add a certain authenticity and help transform even the most modern room. This is particularly so if the room lacks mouldings. Deep skirting boards and wide door frames can add the right tone to a room.

Window treatment is a breeze with country style. Use lace, muslin or floral prints; a little of each if you fancy them together. Shutters are ideal, though considerably more expensive. You might consider using only small ones on lower windows and combine these with simply hung fabric curtains. But remember that the key to the country look is simplicity.

Old pine furniture, well-worn cedar pieces, armoires, sturdy cupboards, and sideboards are all the right things in the country setting. And it's almost a bonus when they happen to carry the scars of age. This idea may require a slight mental adjustment if shiny surfaces of perfect smoothness are what you have previously admired. But if you have children, think of the relief of living with things that have already done noble service, think of not having to be anxious about highly polished furniture being scuffed and scratched by the inadvertent bump. Sturdy old pieces are easy to live with because they've been around a long time and they've been through the wars already.

Because of our relatively small population in early times, really old Australian furniture isn't in abundance, and exceptional pieces will become increasingly rare and consequently more valuable. But if you keep your eyes open you'll be surprised at how often you will happen upon simpler pieces, well-crafted old blanket boxes, rush- and cane-seated chairs and the ubiquitous but virtuous bentwoods. You'll find chests of drawers and old government-issue writing tables that make excellent dining boards.

Another long-observed rule can now be abandoned: things don't need to match. Lovers of the country look won't think it odd or strange if you have a collection of individual dining chairs. The country look, indeed, gives unheard of freedom of choice to the home decorator.

An attractive Italian hand-painted jug filled with exotic flowers is an unusual touch in a country house.

ABOVE
Honest old pieces like this hanging wall cabinet and simple table make a handsome setting for white lilies in an old mug, with a metal water bottle and an antique mortar and pestle as companion pieces.

RIGHT
Simple cedar furniture was made to furnish this slab hut.

CREATING THE COUNTRY LOOK

LEFT
On a bedside table, these family photos in their unusual frames give a nice sentimental touch to an original Federation style room. The soldier pictured in the Australian motif frame served at Gallipoli.

OPPOSITE PAGE
Simplicity is the key to the country style as epitomised here by the curtains of plain sailmaker's cotton canvas and an old dough bin used as a table in the bay window of a bedroom.

As for soft furnishings, again country style makes few demands. Upholstery fabrics can be plain, striped, plaid or floral, and the chairs and sofas can be in any style or shape. Slip covers are a boon and can change the scene quickly. Or you can try a loose fabric throw-over to cover any unsuitable upholstery. Tapes or ties at the corners will help keep them in place. And by the way, a dip into a cold-tea bath will nicely tone down any patterns and colours that seem a bit too vivacious for your laid-back country look.

Baskets are wonder workers in establishing the easy country style. Hand-woven, rough, twig, ethnic, what you will, they're

OPPOSITE
An arrangement of autumn leaves in a stoneware jug perfectly complements the colours used in the large framed pastel drawing hung above the table.

Georgian joinery on a staircase; an example of early carpenters' expertise in building a fine country house with timber milled on site.

CREATING THE COUNTRY LOOK

Mounds of fresh produce heaped on an old table by the kitchen window immediately create the country theme and atmosphere.

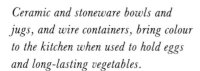

Ceramic and stoneware bowls and jugs, and wire containers, bring colour to the kitchen when used to hold eggs and long-lasting vegetables.

Baskets are wonder workers in a country environment. They can hold so many different things and at the same time display them, adding more colour to the scene. Here, a hand-woven basket from New Guinea holds two kinds of onions at hand for the cook.

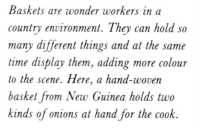

perfect props. Leave them in their natural state; or if they're too battered for your taste, paint them in muted tones of forest green, terracotta or french grey and enjoy their countryfied character. Fill them with potted plants, with a clutch of posies in small vases, with long-lasting vegetables like pumpkins and squash, or with printed fabric pieces that are waiting for your quilting needle. Baskets are meant to hold things; the more decorative the things the better, and the more baskets the merrier in country style.

Cushions are another easy mood-maker. Many attractive ones can be bought. Or you might try your hand at quilting a few cushion covers just to get started on that intriguing craft. Cross-stitch, *petit point* and *gros point*, or crewel work are all ideal means of making a hand-crafted statement that perfects the country look.

For the walls: framed samplers, pretty botanical or animal

In a country kitchen the wood-burning stove has a companion bread oven. Its cosy atmosphere is enlivened by the old Kelim rug on the floor and the warm tones of the table and rush-seated chairs that furnish it.

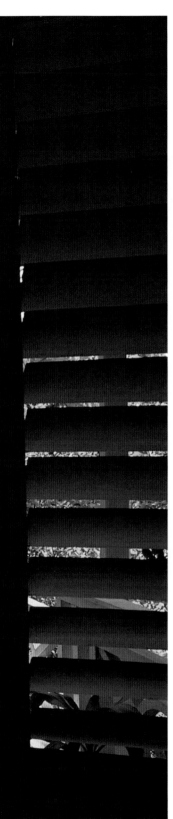

Moveable shuttered doors open out onto a cool veranda. Together, these are the ideal answer to a semi-tropical climate's heat.

prints, faded family photos, and children's drawings all come into their own, as do china and ceramic plates that perhaps have some sentimental family attachment.

Though old things have an important place in the country look, there is also an exciting new aspect to it. Today's craftsmen, carpenters and makers of handmade crafts, are creating articles of virtu that in time will become just as valuable as the rare older objects. We are the lucky ones who can have the pleasure of seeking them out. Though these newly made pieces won't already have done noble service, you can be sure that by the time they have been handed down they too will have taken on the well-weathered but always charming country look.

For a simple answer to ventilation— the combination of open slats with a window above and open railings below.

CREATING THE COUNTRY LOOK

45

New lace panels with an old-time charm were bought by Evelyn Bloom to give an authentic touch to this door of Wollombi House.

An ornate metal gate opens into the garden of a Blue Mountains house.

Lichens, moss and stone are the finer details of the worn entrance steps at the front of this house.

47

ABOVE
Dried rushes in a country waterhole

RIGHT
Afternoon light on autumn leaves

48

COUNTRY COLOURS

THE architect Robin Boyd was once asked how he would suggest making Australia more beautiful. His airy reply was, 'Paint it white.' At the time, in the mid-1970s, when we were going through our Mediterranean period, it seemed like quite a good answer. But our image of ourselves has improved since then. We realise that wasn't at all what we needed.

To make Australia more beautiful, all we need do is reflect and magnify what our country shows us: the colours of earth, the muted smokey blues of far-off mountain ranges, the grey-greens of the eucalypts and the subtle shadings of their striated bark, the sandstone and salmon pinks of rock formations. These are the cohesive colours that beautify our land.

Country colours have a naturally weathered look. They're either bleached by the sun, veiled with a fine layer of dust, or perhaps muted by lichen's growth. They are, in effect, toned down by nature's brush, and that 'softened' look is the one that makes such an impact upon our senses. It gives us the message that we can relax and enjoy the simple things of life.

The growing popularity of country style is due in great part to the effect these subtle colours have on our feeling

ABOVE
Bush rock with traces of iron oxide

LEFT
Scarred and weathered wooden boards

49

of well-being. Think about the peaceful mood a day in the country evokes. These are the colours of nature's palette that create a natural masterpiece, and it's a work of art we're free to copy as we choose.

ABOVE
A terrace row in a country town, South Australia

RIGHT
Detail of the wall of an old slab hut

COUNTRY COLOURS

ABOVE
Sunset's fiery glow, Western Australia

RIGHT
Tomatoes on an Australian pottery plate

COUNTRY COLOURS

LEFT
An old Kelim rug on a cedar floor

BELOW
Polished floor and old linoleum

ABOVE
The peeling bark of a eucalyptus tree

RIGHT
Sandstock bricks make up a garden terrace.

COUNTRY TEXTURES

WHILE the mood of country style is soft and comfortable, not all its textures are. The variety of textures gives a distinctive character to our country theme.

The land itself shows us its many complexities. The trees have an infinite array of textures and shapes, in forms that are wildly distorted or arrow straight. From the sepulchral white of the ghost gum to the tattered motley of the red gum's bark, all around us we see nature's endlessly varied structure.

Each bush rock, from the pitted granite to the water-smoothed pebble and the gritty sandstone, has its own form and texture. And under foot the mosses, ferns and fungus, the lichens and the leaf litter are a bas relief of nature's making.

Even the human creations—sheds, fences, old slab huts holding firmly together over decades of time and discomforting extremes of climate—add their splintery, paint-peeled surfaces to the picture. And so the externals show

LEFT
Much weathered old sliprail fence

55

Dried out and bleached timber flooring

OPPOSITE PAGE
A weathered blue-painted door panel

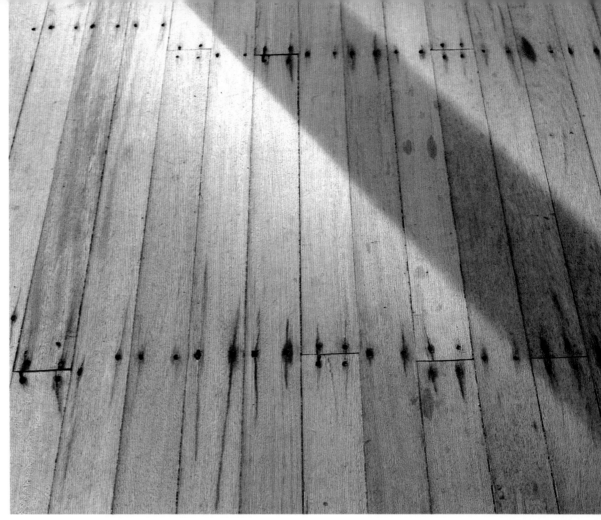

Detail of milled and adzed grey timber

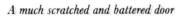

A much scratched and battered door

COUNTRY TEXTURES

57

ABOVE
Grey boulders in sun and shade

LEFT
An old water tank begins to rust

COUNTRY TEXTURES

LEFT
Twin-gabled corrugated iron roof

BELOW
A splintered post and picket gate

RIGHT
A make-do catch for a cupboard door

BELOW
Here, green venetians shade a veranda, while the intricate tracery of metal and wooden features, in white, also look cool.

The fine architectural details on this typical Queensland veranda are magnificently enhanced by sunlight and deep shadow within.

us a deeply weathered face, wrinkled and roughly textured and timeless.

But what translates to interior scenes are the mellower moods of country texture. These are the shapes of wooden grain scoops, the network of reeds in a basket, the grain of an old pine table, the feel of old cotton stitched into quilts, the tissue of handmade lace hung at a window. The tactile fabric of Australian country style is woven on a loom of country textures.

EARLY DAYS

IT is interesting to see how early settlers constructed their houses in the foreign places that were to become their new homelands. The Dutch in the East Indies, the Spanish in Mexico, the Portugese in Macau—all of them had the urge to transpose their native architecture to foreign climes. Some of the transplants took, and others were totally rejected.

In the early days of European settlement in Australia, it was very much a matter of needs must. But wattle-and-daub quickly gave way to clay bricks and hewn stone. It was great good fortune that the Georgian style of architecture was the prescription for this particular transplant. Well-proportioned, symmetrical Georgian buildings were destined to have a long and graceful life, and the advent of the veranda was probably the best possible benefit for an Australian architecture that was truly congruent with its environment.

Early houses of substance generally were fortunate in their settings of large landholdings. Usually they were built in the most advantageous spot to capture expansive vistas of the countryside. We have to turn to old watercolours and oil paintings to see what such places looked like in their original settings. However, many of the houses, even though their estates might have been reduced, remain intact to give us the enjoyment of reliving the past.

In this chapter we visit some splendid examples of the graceful houses that belong to our original country style. Once they were the homes of the new colony's barons—the landed gentry of a past age.

The original hipped roof, steeply pitched at forty-five degrees, was covered by the broken-back medium pitch of the sheet-metal roof tiles of later alterations. Its profile and the deep shaded veranda are the distinctive symbols of the traditional Australian homestead we know so well.

Wrought metal columns have a graceful character, lending a sophisticated style to the verandas of Elizabeth Farm. The deeply and unevenly worn sandstone paving reveals the age of the house. Vines wrap these cool pavilions in seasonal shade and allow winter sunshine to warm them.

In the Beginning

In John Macarthur's bedroom-library, his specially designed writing desk has been perfectly reproduced. This design was executed to his order; the top cupboard sits on the writing table, and the two are separate pieces.

Coir matting on a bare wooden floor is an easygoing floor covering for sitting areas. Furniture with slip covers in fabrics that replicate the textiles used at that time give a simple, low-key character to the sitting room.

BENEATH the corrugated-iron roof of Elizabeth Farm cottage in Parramatta, west of Sydney, are the original timbers and wooden shingles of Australia's oldest house, still there after almost two hundred years. This house has a family history that goes back almost to the first settlement. It was begun in 1793, built by convicts under the owner's supervision. Crudely fired hand-pressed bricks, made from clay dug just a hundred metres from the cottage, were laid with mud mortar. At that time, lime was not readily available.

Built as the home of the Macarthur family, Elizabeth Farm cottage was a starkly functional dwelling. A hipped roof covered with ironbark shingles and small windows gave little hint of the graceful home it would eventually become. In fact, owing to the lack of building knowledge in the colony at that time and the inexperience in dealing with the terrain and climatic extremes, this structure, like many others, very soon began showing signs of instability. By 1817, Elizabeth Macarthur, whose home it was, had written to her family in England, 'The house is tumbling down, it is quite a ruin.'

It is intriguing to wonder why John Macarthur never made the decision to start again from scratch and build an entirely new house for his family. Within several decades of the colony's beginning, tremendous progress in construction techniques had been made, and far superior buildings were being erected. He was not hindered by a shortage of land; by that time he had over sixteen hundred acres at his disposal. The cottage might easily have been repaired and used as an annexe for housing guests, and a more commodious place might have been built for his growing family. Instead, he continued to remodel and extend the original structure.

It seems that Macarthur enjoyed replanning for its own sake and threw himself vigorously into his architectural research for the project. So the unfortunate Elizabeth continued living in a house much too small for their needs and had to put up with the uproar that extensions and rebuilding always create. Happily, the end result, as we see Elizabeth Farm today, makes amends for the distress it must have caused her.

Elizabeth Macarthur was a resourceful and self-sufficient woman. She had to be. The master of the house was gone for long periods at a time, first for four years, after which he

Here, the splendid cedar joinery can be admired for its diversity. The fact that it was entirely handmade in such an unfavourable period of Australia's history makes it all the more admirable.

The original furnishings of Elizabeth Farm are in the possession of John Macarthur's descendants. To restore and furnish the house, each piece was reproduced exactly, so that what we see there today is as close to the original as it is possible to conceive nearly two hundred years after the house was built and furnished.

returned to Australia for the next four years, and then he was away again for another nine years. Through all this Elizabeth managed admirably, though separated from three of her children, who had been sent to England for their education. She remained in charge of the estate with a small household; two little girls, their governess and a few convict servants.

The absence of her husband, who was renowned for his argumentative and volatile character, might have been as much a blessing as a trial for Elizabeth. However, it must have been a much calmer period for her after 1806, when the convict farmer Thomas Herbert, a very capable man, was employed as over-seer and some of the weight of managing this huge property was lifted from Elizabeth's shoulders.

In 1826 and the following year, extensions and alterations to the house were under way again in earnest. Perhaps for once Elizabeth may have voiced some objections; as she wrote to her son Edward, who was still in England, she had been ordered from the house: 'If I return, your father will not proceed.' Later she added, 'I have lived so long in a ruin of a cottage that I think it best that I stay where I am [living with her daughter in Sydney] until I have a bedroom finished.'

And so the house took on its new shape with alterations and

additions designed by the architects Henry Cooper and John Verge. Better materials and the work of skilled craftsmen also added to its refinement. The Australian red cedar joinery was hand wrought, as were the tapered architraves around the front doors, the timber pilasters in the library and the fine framing of interior glass doors. At last Elizabeth Farm had a house that was a gracious home.

Five years later the Macarthurs' son John died in London. Elizabeth had not seen him since he went away to school at the age of seven, thirty years before. The elder John Macarthur's already troubled mental state worsened with his grief. Perhaps to distract himself with frantic activity, he began planning more alterations to the house. But in the following year he was confined to his apartments. His mistrust of everyone increased. Poor Elizabeth, accused of infidelity, was banished. She went to live with her married daughter, Mary, and her husband in Woolloomooloo. In April 1834 John Macarthur, senior, died, after having been declared insane because his manic-depressive condition was deemed ungovernable.

At last Elizabeth was able to return to her 'beloved home' beside the Parramatta River. She had certainly earned her fair share of its peace and prosperity. During her remaining years she was probably grateful for her husband's determination to renovate and improve the house. A charming and graceful home had evolved from the construction site she had endured for so many years.

Elizabeth Farm, so sensitively restored by the Historic Houses Trust of New South Wales, must be considered the antecedent of Australian country style. The house sits easily upon its site, surrounded by a well-planned garden that incorporates all possible vestiges of past plantings. The interior restoration and furnishings, wherever possible an exact replica of the original, have been handled expertly. With obvious regard for the nuances of the period, the rooms are sparely and carefully furnished, for the house never did become opulent in style. Today, visitors might imagine themselves entering a house in which Mrs Macarthur could appear at any moment and invite them to tea.

Two garden rooms, though very small (each less than three metres square), flank the veranda at each end in front of the house. Obviously they were much used and enjoyed as quiet spots for reading or study. Simple linoleum covers the floor of one, while coir matting is used in the other. Cane chairs, muslin curtains and simple cotton prints as slip covers give the rooms a charming atmosphere.

This doorway leads into the children's room, the only room apportioned to them. It may point up the social standing of children in those days, for the room is scantily appointed and unembellished.

John Macarthur's portrait looms above the fireplace of his apartment. This is by far the most elaborately furnished room in the house. He spent more and more time there as his mental condition worsened, so perhaps the fine furnishings may have given him some consolation. The bed has been carefully assembled with the requisite horsehair and feather mattresses of the period, and the furnishing fabrics closely approximate those of his time.

The bedroom of which Elizabeth Macarthur wrote, 'I shall not return until I have a suitable bedroom there.' This calm and pretty room would have been a great solace to the lady who had suffered so much so that her house could be put in order. Here the paint colour, the fabrics and the fine four-poster bed, in a room whose shuttered windows overlook a private patch of garden, surely would have made their mistress happy.

Across its expansive driveway, Lanyon presents a welcoming aspect to the many visitors who come here.

On the shaded veranda, finely woven old cane chairs offer cool comfort on a hot day. The floorboards, so exactly mitred on the corners, are of exceptionally fine grained wood and meticulously finished.

Historic enclave

WHAT could be more typical of Australian country than a sheep property beside the Murrumbidgee River? Nothing, perhaps, except the house called Lanyon that sits upon that property.

It was built on a grant of land in the Tharwa region, not far from Canberra, the property being named after one of its original co-owners, John Lanyon. In the beginning there was just a group of rude slab huts that housed fifty people. Later came a small cottage in the form of a belltower, and even a barracks building for the convict labourers. Then in 1860 the new owner, Andrew Cunningham, built the graceful single-storey house that can be seen, in part, today. It was built of rubble coated with stucco and had a wide, wooden-floored veranda on two sides. Tall french doors opened out from well-proportioned rooms. It was a house that had the very imprint of what we now consider Australian country style.

The Cunningham family were to live there for more than sixty-six years. In 1905 they needed more space, and a new wing was added. But everything else remained unchanged. The dairy, blacksmith's shop, other cottages—all the buildings that formed a satellite group—made a courtyard at the back of the house. The kitchen too, as was the custom, stood apart from the main house.

The simplicity of style and basic utilitarian character of the homestead complex make this a prime example of our early country buildings. And it is also a rich example, since outbuildings rarely survive intact to tell the full story of homestead life. The old bunya pines towering beside the homestead and the garden that abuts it are a living reminder of the life-sustaining qualities of such fine old houses.

Lanyon speaks volumes for the stability and industry of country people and, in its way, communicates a sense of history in the making. Since the property was bought by the government in 1975, it has been painstakingly restored. Using every possible documentation and first-hand account, the National Trust has ensured its authenticity and its future.

Gravel, raked with the finesse of a Japanese garden's style, gives an unusually aesthetic aspect to this expansive open space.

ABOVE
A detail of the fine joinery finish of the cedar french doors.

LEFT
The trunk of an old bunya pine bulks large beyond the veranda posts. Above the french doors, transom lights illuminate the adjoining rooms.

ABOVE
Old linoleum has the intricate pattern and cool colour of antique Persian ceramic tiles.

ABOVE
On the classically simple top of a cedar chiffonier an ornate gilded Victorian jug holds a bouquet of mixed bulbs and wildflowers.

LEFT
While the occasional piece of furniture may seem primitive, the overall style of Lanyon was quite sophisticated for its time and place. The wood-lined walls in this room have a painted finish.

76

RIGHT
A long, narrow hall has a cool, patterned linoleum runner. Doors that open on either side seem to have been spaced so that natural light illuminates the whole passage.

OPPOSITE

The living room's sunny aspect gives onto views of rolling green paddocks, old trees, and, further off, the bush itself. The fine cedar joinery, which was milled from trees on the property, along with the room's excellent proportions, make a fitting setting for Arthur Boyd's striking painting.

RIGHT

The old slab hut faces the main house across a dark pond.

The art of living

TUCKED away in the bush near the Shoalhaven River on the south coast of New South Wales, Bundanon sits amid green pastures under the shadow of Pulpit Rock. This graceful, late Georgian house hardly shows its 125 years. At times in its history it has been abandoned, uncared for, even used as a hay storage shed—incredible to think so now that it has been returned to its former state of simple splendour. Its sandstone blocks have been cleaned; inside, the floors and walls have been sympathetically restored. Now it gives the impression of never having known lean times. Large, well-proportioned rooms in an uncomplicated architectural plan of four up, four down are furnished in comfortable and unaffected style. Fine old pieces team with chintz-covered chairs and, underfoot, the rich jewel colours of old oriental rugs.

The Shoalhaven River makes its presence felt with the occasional flood, though it is a good kilometre away and cannot be seen from the house. Nearly two hundred years ago, when George Bass had to manoeuvre his whaleboat through its treacherous delta, he observed that he did not like the narrow entrance, so filled with mud and streaked with sandspits that he could give it 'no better name than Shoal Haven'. However, the present owner of Bundanon, painter Arthur Boyd, has found rich inspiration in this riverscape.

This part of the New South Wales south coast was opened up to cattle grazing by Alexander Berry in 1822. Fifteen years later the Bundanon crown land grant was taken up. The original dwelling, a slab hut, still stands, with the help of some restoration which faithfully followed its simple structure. There is an intriguing anomaly here, for the hut seems to have been planned for grander dimensions; its fireplace is manor-sized, beautifully crafted in sandstone, seemingly built to be used from the back as well as the front. Its hearth is so generous that a fully fledged fire in the grate would create such heat that it would drive any occupant from the tiny hut. Perhaps this may

The graceful little cottage which is now the kitchen wing.

Bundanon, cloaked in deep afternoon shade cast by its sheltering old magnolia tree, has an air of being in a past, more peaceful time.

have been the first site planned for the main house but abandoned for the more pleasant aspect on the opposite hill.

There are other buildings on the property that predate the main house. A weatherboard cottage, now used as the kitchen wing, was built in the 1840s. A wooden walkway joins it to a twin structure, currently the guest wing, and these two are linked by a covered walkway to the main house and sheltered by a venerable wisteria vine.

The sandstone main house was built in 1866, as the legend carved above the door proclaims. Its stone was quarried on the property, and its joinery made of cedar. In front there is a veranda with tall wooden pillars at ground level; the upstairs balcony, with its sharply sloping roof, gives a pleasant cosiness to the bedroom outlook.

In the corner a highly gilded, ornate oriental writing cabinet makes an interesting contrast to the bold modern ceramic plate by Arthur Boyd.

It was love at first sight when Arthur Boyd and his wife, Yvonne, first saw Bundanon on a brief visit in January 1972. They had been invited by its then owner, Sydney art dealer Frank McDonald, to spend a weekend there. In the early 1970s McDonald and his Sydney partner bought the property— unkempt paddocks surrounded by stony hills and a house that had seen better times. In due course a garden was planted, and the paddocks were made orderly again. It had already begun its return to serenity when the Boyds first saw it. And on that first visit Arthur Boyd took a canvas down to the riverside to paint. It was a hot, windy day; the heat was such that the pigment melted on his palette. But the painting, called *River Bank*, is now in the National Gallery, Canberra. Many more paintings were to follow over the years, and the river would become one of his prime inspirations.

What Arthur and Yvonne Boyd realised was that they liked the area so much they wanted to return. Soon after, they found a property near by, and Earie Park became their haven by the river for a time.

Because the area had long been an inspiration to various famous Australian artists, starting with Conrad Martens, then Elioth Gruner and later Lloyd Rees, McDonald and his partner tried, unsuccessfully, to interest the New South Wales government in making a regional gallery of the old house. Though it was a plausible suggestion, logistics were against the scheme; the property was just too inaccessible. So when in 1977 their submission failed, the disappointed owners put the property up for sale. Boyd, in London, heard of the proposed sale and by telephone, telegram and letter kept in contact with events. He begged McDonald not to sell until he had the chance to bid. At last, the artist and his family were able to buy the house that had won their hearts at their first encounter with it.

Much of the life of the river area has been recorded by Arthur Boyd during the years spent at Bundanon. The location of his first painting was once the landing stage of the Bundanon

EARLY DAYS

*Entrancing portraits of the Boyds'
daughter Polly are the focal point of
an upstairs bedroom. Her serious
little face gives a touch of whimsy.*

*In the same upstairs bedroom an
unusual collection of feathers graces the
top of an antique chest of drawers*

*An elegant cedar washstand adds a
touch of class to a basic old white
enamel bathtub in the spacious room
upstairs that has been converted into a
bathroom-cum-dressing room.*

ferry. One winter the ferry was carried by floodwaters high among the trees on the riverbank and its great white bulk grounded there. During another flood a neighbour used a helicopter to try to herd this cattle to dry land. Happenings like these sometimes find their way into Boyd's paintings. Through them we see the rich pageant of the river's seasonal changes.

The Boyds have hardly tampered with the simple grace of Bundanon but have made it into an abundantly welcoming home. They have given it an air of lived-in comfort while at the same time adding the lively character of a gallery, with pottery, sculpture and paintings by every member of the creative Boyd family on display.

Almost to his own surprise Arthur Boyd has become one of the largest landholders in the district. However, the property is simply the setting for a most prized jewel, the graceful house Bundanon, which, the owner has announced, will be a bequest to the people of Australia.

EARLY DAYS

*The library shelves hold not only books
but a wide selection of Boyd family
pottery pieces, ranging from the naive
to the sophisticated.*

'The Boyds have hardly tampered with the simple grace of Bundanon but have made it into an abundantly welcoming home'

LEFT AND BELOW
The stairway's form is illuminated by light sources at two levels. The second flight leads across a wide hall to french doors that open onto a cool veranda, overlooking the old magnolia.

ABOVE
Through the window of the slab hut, a glimpse of the interior.

OPPOSITE
The old slab hut stands alone on the opposite hill, sheltered by trees.

ABOVE
A detail of Bundanon's sandstone blocks and a deeply embrasured window.

LEFT
A french door seen across the weathered front veranda boards.

OPPOSITE
In the garden, which gives much pleasure with its fruit and flowers, a sculptured figure by Guy Boyd can be seen half hidden by greenery.

Familiar values

WHEN Castlemaine was little more than a settlement of gold seekers living in rough temporary dwellings, a solid house was built there. Two years later, in 1859, it was sold and renamed Buda, after its new owner's native Budapest. From that time until 1981, when it was bequeathed to the people of Victoria, the house remained the home of the Leviny family. The last surviving daughter, before she died in her nineties, willed the state this treasure. It is indeed a gift rarer than gold, for it encapsulates the history of a family from a time when rough goldrush settlements became towns and then turned into cities.

The furnishings and artefacts in Buda today are all those used by the Levinys, so we have at once a true picture of the life and changing times of an Australian country town. These are the kinds of things that grace our country theme today. Seeing them *in situ* gives us an awareness we otherwise might never have of such a family's life.

Ernest Leviny was not an average prospector on the gold-fields. In fact, he would have been a man of unusual talents in any situation. Born in Hungary, he was already an established goldsmith when he made his decision to go prospecting in

A finely marbled mantel was the focus of this living room. How many maids came running at the sound of the imperious little hand bell?

OPPOSITE PAGE
A splendidly embroidered firescreen was no doubt the handiwork of one of Ernest Leviny's talented daughters.

RIGHT

This beautifully crafted garden gate with its contrasting treillage is a wonderful example of the craftsmanship of a past, golden age.

BELOW

The very grand pediment and columns at the entrance to Buda seem to belong to a much more pretentious building than this house with its corrugated metal roof.

OPPOSITE

Because Ernest Leviny was a keen bird fancier, the aviaries he had built were particularly fine, their style reflecting the delicate lines of those in the Europe of his youth.

OPPOSITE PAGE
This art nouveau lamp was probably a great favourite with the Levinys in the early 1900s. The attractive cedar dressing-table beneath the window holds soapstone carvings that may have been mementoes of an overseas trip for someone in the family.

RIGHT
The dining room's austere furnishing is softened by the light from the windows, which were surprisingly large for their era. The hard, paved flooring gives a slightly puritanical air to the room.

Australia. Unlike most prospectors, he arrived on the goldfields well prepared. Not only did he bring special mining equipment with him; he had a crew of labourers as well. What he wasn't prepared for was that his labourers would quickly desert him to go digging for themselves.

He soon decided to leave the harsh conditions of the fields to others and opened a shop. Business was booming in gold-mad Castlemaine. Working as a watchmaker and jeweller, in no time at all he prospered. Soon he began dealing in real estate as well and quickly became a respected citizen in the burgeoning town. It was then he bought his house.

Ernest married and in time raised a large family. As the family grew, Buda, like many of today's family homes, was renovated and extended. It had not been built as a grand house, but as it stood on two hectares there was plenty of room for expansion. Ernest's children were creative, and he encouraged them to develop their talents, even designing and building studio rooms for their artistic projects. The daughters' embroidery and enamel-on-metal work are among the family artefacts that furnish the house still.

Surrounding the house is a garden planned by Ernest under the friendly guidance of that period's government botanist, Baron Ferdinand von Mueller. This garden, planted with old-fashioned flowers and shrubs, redolent of another era, is unique. Because of the family's dedication to it, the garden's design was not tampered with, and the original plan, well over a hundred years old, survives to this day. Aviaries were built in the garden, for Ernest Leviny was a keen bird fancier. The grounds must have been a lovely setting for the garden parties the family held there.

OPPOSITE
*A detail of another bedroom shows the
bedside table with the everyday items
of a less complicated age.*

LEFT
*In earlier times the tester bed would
have had its share of flounces or
drapery. And, obviously, richer
hangings once graced the high window.
But as in every family home,
circumstances change over time, and
this may have been the look of later
years in this busy home.*

BELOW
*A detail of the dressing-table shows it
as it looked when the family
entertained and dressed up for a garden
or dinner party.*

While Ernest Leviny encouraged his childrens' creative interests and gave them great freedom to follow those interests, he
seems to have discouraged them from marrying and leading
their own lives. Young men who called were never considered
suitable for his talented daughters. But it is because some daughters never married, and the estate did not have to be split up to
be shared among their families, that Buda remains with us
today. This fine example of a family home, in a town whose
country origins were formed by the discovery of gold, would not
have remained as a perfect remembrance of things past.

All the implements for baking would have been kept at the ready. No doubt many a rich pastry would have been made here, and the cauldron would have bubbled with caraway soup in the cold winter months.

The kitchen was a busy spot. Imagine the hubbub of preparations for a garden party or formal dinner. The crocks, pots and rainwater tank at the back door would have been in constant use on such busy days.

EARLY DAYS

'The furnishings and artefacts in Buda today are all those used by the Levinys, so we have at once a true picture of the life and changing times of an Australian country town'

The veranda's wide, shaded overhang gives an area for entertaining and enjoying the breezes that can be life-saving on hot days. And when nights are sweltering too, the veranda often becomes a sleep-out; on one side there's an old four-poster, as well as a linen hammock, offering a place to sleep when it's too warm for comfort indoors.

Unchanged through the years

IN a valley west of Sydney there is a historic settlement where one of the oldest houses has stood, almost unaltered, for over a hundred years. The men who built the house were brothers, George and William Harris. One of them supervised the quarrying of the sandstone blocks from the surrounding hills, the other the milling of local timber for the cedar joinery. When the house was finished it became for seventeen years the shared family home of the brothers and their expanding families. In time there were twelve children living under its shingled roof. Since it isn't a very big house, they must have shared very close quarters. But there was plenty of land around them on which to play; the property spreads for hectares under the shadow of Mount Misery, standing aloof and cloud-shrouded in an otherwise sunny landscape.

Over the years, other owners came and went. In the 1930s the original shingled roof was replaced by one of corrugated iron. The garden changed and grew. One owner put in a tennis court; another allowed it to become derelict; later still, the court's space gave way to a man-made lake created by the present owners, Sheila Carroll and Denis Allard.

The year 1868 chiselled in stone above the door bears witness to the age of the house. More than anything else, the stone-flagged veranda, worn by the tread of many feet, shows its age. But the thick sandstone walls remain implacably solid, despite the house's changing fortunes. Perhaps the worst times were when, left untenanted, its deserted veranda offered shelter to grazing cattle wandering at will around the house and taking cover when needed under its generous overhang.

The garden, since the present owners moved in, has had a few dead trees replaced, some minor clearing has been done, and the lake's abundant rushes have been kept in check by the

One of the three attic windows that grace the steeply pitched roof of this 1868 sandstone farmhouse. The startling contrast of red iron roof and bright blue sky is the essence of Australian country, which this house, the home of Sheila Carroll and painter Denis Allard, exemplifies.

This room acts as an office-cum-workroom where Sheila Carroll can spin her natural sheep's wool or telephone her friends. Big baskets full of uncarded natural wool look right at home awaiting the spinner.

occasional burning off. But generally the setting remains simple and unfussed, surroundings that suit the old house perfectly.

A cluster of old plum trees arch over the back veranda, where many wonderful finds are kept, for Sheila Carroll is an avid collector of Australiana, and though no longer engaged professionally, she hasn't lost her eye for the rare and wonderful object. The back veranda connects the old soot-blackened kitchen to the Stranger's Room (so called because it had no inner door into the house and was accessible only to the veranda) and the Lovers' Room, now a hideaway, a cosy place with a four-poster bed and a big open fireplace. This room probably once was the family dining room, for it is located conveniently close to the kitchen.

Sheila Carroll lives in and loves this place with the restraint and sympathy to leave it in its original state. 'My daughter used to walk across the paddock to the one-teacher school until the time came for her to go off to boarding school. And even though we've been here for twenty years, we're practically newcomers compared with many families living in the area. Some of them go back three or four generations,' she says.

As we admire the lake and the ducks and geese on it, a black swan appears, skimming the water. 'He just flew in one day, about three years ago. He gets along well with the others, and so he just stayed on.' And then she observes that the reeds, lately burnt off, are growing back fast. We come to the pomegranate tree, one of its limbs almost touching the ground. 'It's very old,' she says. 'We're undecided whether to cut off the drooping side or just let it be.'

Showing us through the house, she says, 'What's that old saying—once a collector, always a collector?' and admits that she finds it very hard to part with certain things. She points to an old meat-safe which is about to be given away. It's going to her son, so she knows it will have a caring home. Only under such circumstances is she willing to let things go.

Some distance away the traffic can be seen buzzing by on the main road. But here, with the setting sun glowing on the sandstone, it is as peaceful as it must have been on that afternoon in 1868 when George and William Harris moved in with their wives and children to celebrate their housewarming.

Under the generous overhang of the back veranda, a veritable treasure-trove of old country things is stored beneath bunches of drying herbs and flowers. No doubt, when this was a bustling family home, the back veranda would have been the hub of activities.

At the foot of an old iron-and-brass bedstead, a kerosene-tin chest of drawers looks surprisingly smart. How innovative our early settlers were, making use of all the basic things that came their way: flour bags, boxes and crates, and most of all, kerosene tins.

BELOW
A charming corner of an attic bedroom has a graceful wicker chair placed invitingly beside the open window.

EARLY DAYS

108

In one of the attic bedrooms an old rustic chest of drawers is a reminder of the making-do of past times. Put together without the cabinet-maker's skill or the ability to finish smoothly, this piece shows the honest enterprise of an unskilled hand-worker. His tools for the job would have been limited, but his interpretation, given the materials at his disposal, was a unique artisan achievement.

109

*An old plum tree in bloom, the
essential water tank, the outbuildings
sheltering under their tangled canopy of
vines—these are particulars of an
unmistakably Australian country style.*

On the fence post of the property a carved wooden crane stands guard at the gate. The lake was excavated by Denis Allard on a spot where a tennis court once stood. Now the reflection of Mount Misery makes a wonderful counterpoint to the simple arch of a wooden bridge and the uprights of reeds that soften the lake's edge.

The magistrates' house

FROM outside it looks just like a child's drawing of a small cottage. But inside it surprises you with its generous living space. It is almost impossible to believe that the house has four bedrooms, let alone a formal dining room, a library, and more.

The house was originally built to accommodate the magistrates of the Touring Court on their judicial rounds. Naturally such a residence needed to be a cut above the average cottage. Even so, the exterior was kept low key, without ostentation of any kind. While it presents an impeccable front, the sandstone blocks being examples of the finest stonemasons' craft, the blocks forming the building's sides are considerably rougher than those of the façade. The house appears also to have had three front doors. It's hard to guess what sort of segregation this implies, but they must have had their purpose.

The earliest staircase leading to the top storey went up from the living room. Traces of its original position remain in the patched ceiling boards. For many years now, access to the upstairs has been by way of a steep flight of stairs off the kitchen area at the back of the house.

Though it is on a smallish scale, the house does show its Georgian ancestry in the traditional symmetry of the style. The very deep window and door embrasures have cedar panelling, but the owners, Michael Pritchard and Dean Kempnick, decided to paint them. 'It was going to be a terrible job to take them back to the original,' says Michael Pritchard, 'But more importantly, we like the look of painted finishes. Lots of people suggested that we take the interior back to the original sandstone. But we discounted that idea, because it's a Georgian residence, not a rustic country cottage, and it was designed to have a bit of refinement. That's why we decided to give it a little bit more finish.'

The new owners must hardly have known where to begin when faced with the tangle of blackberries outside and an

OPPOSITE PAGE
A splendid old oak dresser holds a rich array of collectibles together with many utilitarian pieces. The blue willow china is a modern copy, but the large serving dish is an original piece. Just some of the owners' collection of *salt-glazed pitchers join ranks with a few modern Pillivuyt lidded casseroles. The Victorian hanging lamp illuminates an Australian cedar pedestal table and loose-covered canvas director's chairs.*

ABOVE
An early Australian kitchen cupboard, made from lining boards, stands against a rough-hewn sandstone wall. Dried hydrangea blooms add interesting texture and colour in a modern cast-concrete footed bowl. The *two nineteenth-century primitive oil paintings of quinces and pomegranates on the wall were painted on the backs of wooden Libby's asparagus packing cases. The cast-iron candelabrum is modern but very suitable.*

The archetypal cottage, red-roofed and
all, it is certainly larger than it looks.
The white picket fence has a dense row
of blue and white agapanthus blooms
in season—'one of the few things that
were worth keeping, after we'd taken
out the mass of blackberries,' say the
owners.

A lake with a summerhouse-cum-folly
were part of the plan to make the
garden resemble a park. It was recently
finished at the time this photograph
was taken and still looked a trifle new,
but it will take on a mellow look
quickly enough. In the meantime, the
owners think it looks its best at night
with the lights that lead up to it giving
it a romantic atmosphere. On a
moonlit night it's an enchanting and
quite ethereal sight.

EARLY DAYS

The front veranda still has its original flooring, parched and quite splintered with long years of use. But it has been left untouched as a reminder of the busy days when the visiting magistrates were in residence.

The unifying aspect of colour is obvious in the formal dining room where no sign of modernity intrudes. There are no electric lights here, just an old oil lamp on the wall and overhead a crystal chandelier of the kind once hung from massive trees to light the festivities of the raj in Indian gardens by night. On the side table are nine remaining Georgian wine glasses from a set of twelve. The cedar table seats ten. The chairs are Georgian, as is the covered silver serving dish.

interior that had been left to fend for itself over many years of casual tenanting. The blackberries had taken over and were four and a half metres high in spots. 'We didn't even know there was fencing in the driveway,' Michael says, 'and we only discovered what was there after we chopped out all the black-berries. Instead of poisoning them and having to wait three months for them to die back, we did it in a weekend.'

There were only a huge old oak and a few big gumtrees on the property at the time. 'We bought a lot of advanced trees and had bulldozers dig holes big enough to plant them,' Dean explains. 'So all the pines, cypress, the bay tree, every single tree of any size, we've planted.' It is an amazing achievement; the garden is certainly in a very altered state from the time when grass grew two metres tall all over the property. They've transformed it from a wilderness to a park in a very short time.

Beside the front door, the tall William and Mary clock, a hall table in oak which dates from the seventeenth century, and an Australian Georgian-period chair are grouped beneath an English portrait of the nineteenth century. A handsome setting.

The splendid rosewood four-poster is a memento of the days of the raj. Its passage from India was no doubt made easier by the fact that the long iron bolts holding it together can be loosened by a large metal key and the whole thing dismantled.

A fine Victorian-era reproduction of a Jacobean oak cupboard has handsome door furnishings in brass and a well-turned rail back. Small oriental boxes and chests are clustered for better viewing under the lamp's light.

Michael and Dean have filled the house with a fine collection of antique furnishings, mostly sophisticated pieces that look very much at home in the stylish interior they've created. But there are areas where simpler, more rustic pieces do have their place. Just as their garden has been planned to have the character of a park, so the house too has been refurbished to recreate the appeal of a past age.

In the upstairs hall an early Australian cedar serving table, circa 1880, holds an early Australian deedbox, a large nineteenth-century ginger jar, and a modern carved duck. Caroline Berry painted the still life on the lining-board wall.

EARLY DAYS

ABOVE
This joyous autumn colour is the reward for long years of planting by each successive owner of the garden. Masses of bulbs and deciduous trees, now in their prime, make a lovely frame for the driveway all year.

FAR RIGHT
The doll's-house veranda of this timber cottage, so gracefully sheltered by tree ferns, has art nouveau brackets that were designed and made by the owner.

RIGHT
On a sunny day this old wooden garden seat offers a quiet place from which to enjoy a sea of jonquils.

SETTINGS PRETTY

IN the gardens of the earliest settlers, edible plants would surely have had priority. Imagine how welcome, and valuable, those first crops must have been. But before long these early settlers must have longed for gardens that would brighten their lives with the colour and perfume of flowers. It's certain that the man of means would have wanted to plant a handsome garden to complement the substantial house he was already planning. Cottage gardens may do for the ordinary folk, but a wealthy citizen demanded something much grander. Probably neither segment of society cared much for the native flowers around them; their unfamiliar conformations were as strange and foreign as the land itself.

For us today, either as admirers or as gardeners ourselves, the wide variety of plants and garden styles is what makes our country gardens such a joy. With a generally forgiving climate, we're able to grow such a diversity of things that in one garden we may have exotics from both tropical and colder zones growing alongside the drought-resistant, alkaline-accepting native plants.

ABOVE
*The graceful sweep of this gravel
driveway introduces the visitor to
Buda's beautiful garden in
Castlemaine, Victoria.*

OPPOSITE PAGE
*This garden is well over a hundred
years old, and its long-established trees
testify to the careful planning of the
estate by its owner, Ernest Leviny.*

Trees, fortunately, seem always to have been planted
first in gardens of any size. Of the large indigenous ones,
the Moreton Bay fig and the Norfolk and bunya pines
seem to have been great favourites. It must have been
their scale that appealed, for in size they are reminders of
the oaks and elms of England, those princely sentinels of
lordly acres.

In many cases the antipodean lordly acres today have
become subdivisions, whittled away over the years and
their land allocated to other uses. But many of the original
trees survive as reminders of those early years of great
expectations. The smaller shrubs and plants were swept
away, but luckily their seeds were not entirely scattered
and spent.

For the keen gardener today, establishing a country
garden is not necessarily an uphill battle. With the
reawakened interest in old plants, many nurseries are

OPPOSITE PAGE
The lush growth of hollihocks and violas may conjure up thoughts of an English garden, but the robust clump of amaryllis hints at a much warmer climate, and the peeling bark of the gumtree indicates that it is an Australian garden. This is the garden at Elizabeth Farm, whose replanting has been the result of enthusiastic and careful research.

RIGHT
Agapanthus and wisteria make a lush green and lilac frame for the impressively high sandstone wall of the oak-tree court at Elizabeth Farm, Parramatta, New South Wales.

catering for this interest. Creating a garden with the character of a bygone age needs only good planning and time's indulgence. To quote the writer Beverley Nichols, 'It is only to the garden that time is a friend, giving each year more than he steals.'

We see the truth of this when we admire the gardens that are adjuncts to our country houses. Clearly, it has needed time to establish them, or taken time to rehabilitate them; and now, for our pleasure we must make time to enjoy them, for many are open to the public. There is much to learn just by looking at old gardens, and the keen gardener always hurries home with inspiration to improve his or her own small plot.

Gardens are rewarding things. They make the pretty settings that enhance the character of a house that's welcoming, lived-in and loved.

These old-fashioned roses tumble
attractively over a split-wood fence.
They make a lovely transition from a
more formal garden near the house to
the paddocks and bush that
surround it.

The garden of Wollombi House is once
more perfumed with old-fashioned
roses which the owner has so lovingly
re-established there.

A magnificent bloom from Clarissa Mort's rose allée. Roses, violets, rosemary and and other plants flourish there. Clarissa comes naturally by her gardening skill; her parents' well-loved garden, at their former home, Kennerton Green, was renowned.

*At Bundanon, venerable coral trees
throw their dense shade over the grassy
paddock. In bloom they are a magnet
for flocks of birds.*

'It is only to the garden that time is a friend, giving each year more than he steals'

With the misty blue vistas of the Southern Highlands behind it, an old garden swing suspended from the branch of a tall oak tree invites a moment of repose. This garden has been given a parklike quality by its owners' discerning planting.

TODAY'S COUNTRY

AUSTRALIANS have always prided themselves on their ability to confront difficult situations with native initiative and to make do. It is, perhaps, the one national trait to which we are still prepared to refer with pride. That the children of the television age may lose that facility is one of our sacrifices to the age of electronics.

Perhaps self-sufficiency is simply the currency of young countries. But it continued to be the characteristic of country people in Australia. And when times were tough, happily the facility seemed to resurface in city folk; it had not become a lost art. The McAlpine Collection of Bush Furniture and Toys, which was on display at Sydney's Powerhouse Museum in 1990, amply demonstrated this wonderful, witty spirit of making do.

Today, in the materialistic society, the need to make something from nothing no longer arises. But the Australian Dream, the desire to own your own home on your own quarter-acre, persists as strongly as ever. For those who have taken it a step further, living in the country has become their dream. And to achieve that dream has meant having to plan, to renovate, to build. From a distance maybe it all looks easy. But, in fact, to make their dreams reality required good deal of effort and the summoning up of the best of their initiative to make a home in today's country.

The unforgiving terrain posed its own set of problems, yet the result is one of unusual harmony between quite disparate conventions. Note how the building's lines seem to be an extension of the land's topography. The pitch of the roof appears absolutely congruent with the terrain itself.

The strong profile of this Glenn Murcutt house shows how well his concern for the character of the terrain has been taken into account. The metal structure takes on a surprising lightness and elegance in the butterfly curve of its roof structure.

In the vernacular

GLENN MURCUTT has been the designer of some of our most striking architecture in his quest to create a vernacular style for today's Australian country house. A few years ago he was asked to design a holiday place for a family who had enjoyed camping on a particular site for years and now wanted a structure reminiscent of the carefree tents they'd used. The house he designed has been likened to 'a butterfly alighted'.

Such an ephemeral simile bears little relation to the harsh realities imposed by the site's rugged terrain. It is certain that the architect approached the brief with his customary earnest appraisal of the factors involved. The site, on a windswept slope on the New South Wales south coast, is unforgiving; barren and almost treeless, it is terrain that demands a bold response.

The decision to use structural steel and corrugated sheeting might seem like folly considering the corrosive nature of such a site. But safeguards in jointing procedures, impervious pro-tective coverings and manufacturers' guarantees ensured the longevity of these materials.

Although the interior design is as spare as a nomad's tent, the comfort factor is high. Internally operated blinds can be retracted, angled or closed tight against the light. Insect mesh is a necessary protection against the intrusion of flies and mosquitoes. With no town water laid on, a system was installed to collect rainwater from the roof's main gutter and store it in huge underground tanks.

Glenn Murcutt says, 'I wanted the building to be able to survive well. I felt it had to be simple in form with a gentle roof. I also wanted the roof to feel that it was in flight and very light.' He has succeeded in building a remarkable structure, and his clients love it. The house won the Robin Boyd Award for the best residential project in 1985, and it obviously sets new standards for the Australian country house of the future.

OPPOSITE

*The kitchen benches unobtrusively line
one wall, and the rooms leading out of
the living area take on the look of an
arcade which extends the feeling of
space in a dramatic way, so that the
eye tends always to look beyond the
walls that encompass each area.*

ABOVE

*Inside, the flooring of sand-coloured
tiles is a visual extension of the land's
colour. The effect of light and shade
gives a very interesting tonal contrast
to the monochromatic scheme. This
effect is enhanced by sun shining
through the slatted shade devices.*

133

*The subtle colours of interior walls
and doorways again create the feeling
of large spaces. The arching ceiling
structure gives a grand architectural
openness above eye level. The simple
furnishings have the effect of
understatement in these rooms.*

Heating within the house, which has a high solar input, is boosted by a pot-bellied stove at one end and a built-in fireplace, which radiates heat into both the living area and the master bedroom adjoining it.

OPPOSITE PAGE

The roof beams rise steeply above the long open-plan bedroom area. These beams, together with the frame, were the first things erected. Once the roof was raised, there was plenty of covered space in which to set out mud bricks to be dried, and later these were made into walls.

RIGHT

The steeply pitched attic roof and wide overhang of the veranda are elements that give the house its snug, sheltering look. Built on a rise in the shade of an old gumtree, the house seems to have been there for a very long time.

Homemade

HERE is a house that immediately evokes respect, admiration and, let's confess it, a certain feeling of envy. Deep down in all of us there's an urge to create our own shelter. The closest most of us get to fulfilling this urge is to daydream about it or make and unmake plans. But Wendy Kelly is a lady who has actually built her own home. And this doesn't mean that she used sub-contractors while overseeing the whole affair herself. 'I worked as a builder's labourer,' she says with a smile as she explains how she and her family built their own home.

First the foundation and posts were erected to support a wooden loft. Then, in just eight days, they made two thousand mud bricks, which were spread out to dry under the shelter of the wooden roof that was already in place. The structural frame was built to be load bearing; that is, the mud-brick walls do not support the superstructure. It was designed so that someone who wasn't exactly *au fait* with the mysteries of plumb-lines and uprights could do a reasonable job of laying bricks. By butting them against existing posts, even an amateur could confidently expect to build straight brick walls.

Though the building of the house took about five years all told, that extended time was mainly due to family emergencies and interruptions. 'The actual time to erect the house was eighteen months,' Wendy says. The floor was laid with pavers, all of them seconds. 'Very inexpensive—about half the cost of a concrete slab at that time,' Wendy explains. There is only one new window in the whole house. 'And that was made to match the old ones we had found. Three very nice ones from the demolition of an old school; others from the tip. The arched ones upstairs, interestingly enough, came from an abandoned *pise* house.'

The house plan is a simple, long rectangular shape in which one end is devoted to the service area: laundry and shower recess, with the toilet and handbasin in a separate enclosure. These all back on to the commodious pantry and kitchen so the plumbing is integrated at that end of the house. Upstairs, under a steeply pitched roof, is the sleeping loft. This open space, running the length of the house, could easily be divided into four bedrooms if so desired. Under the exposed beams the walls

LEFT
*Together with the wood-burning stove
in the open kitchen at the far end of the
room, this free-standing iron stove
gives a pleasant warmth to what is a
considerable space. The insulating
qualities of mud brick make this form
of construction heat efficient.*

BELOW

In the kitchen, the clever recycling of an old dresser top gives storage space for serving bowls, old bottles and Wendy's collection of cookbooks. A batch of spicy, oven-warm biscuits on the table suggests that cookbooks are well used in this household.

LEFT

At each end of the bedroom area, which stretches the full length of the house, two tall arched windows give views over the valley below. The floor here, unlike the ground floor, has carpet, but furnishing is minimal. This has the effect of enhancing the architectural aspect of the interior.

have wooden lining boards. At each end, wide arched windows give on to valley views.

Ground-floor walls are unlined and unpainted. The adobe's natural colour is a warm apricot tone which might easily have been created for any of today's most stylish paint charts. The paved floor has been left in its natural state, and rugs are scattered in the sitting areas for added warmth and comfort. A single, free-standing fuel stove provides generous heating for the living area, and the kitchen stove at the far end gives added warmth; thus the whole open space is kept cosy in winter.

It is hard to imagine a more satisfying house; homemade in a style that is the very essence of Australian country, with its corrugated-iron roof and wide shady veranda on three sides. But most intriguingly of all, its substance is the very earth itself.

OPPOSITE

The dining area has a sheltered aspect on the south-facing side. On that corner of the house a small wrap-around conservatory is created by banks of glass louvres, which can be angled to allow a given amount of ventilation.

RIGHT

The core construction of the house is two storeys high, and a terrace opens on the sheltered sides of the house. Sunshine floods in from that aspect. The river flows below the front elevation, and at the back a low hill shelters the building on the eastern side. It is obvious that no detail of the effect of wind and weather has been overlooked in building here.

Solar considerations

ON the Southern Highlands of New South Wales, where winters can be chilly, this modern country house was planned by its owners to take advantage of every ray of sunshine that came its way. As well, it was carefully planned to be as energy efficient as possible.

As it stands today, the house is 'the result of plan number seven', says Lyndsay Pratt, the owner. The architect was first asked to include a large kitchen so that the owners could use it for their catering business. At that point the plan was a kind of U-shape, but 'that ended up looking like an airport terminal'. So it was back to the drawing board—again and again. From the final plan a model was made and at last construction could begin and the house took shape.

Heating was to be of prime importance, so the sunless south side has no windows and the house is positioned with open aspects to the north, west and east so that the sun is captured at all times of the day. And because south-west winds prevail, the glasshouse corner acts as both a visual green spot all year long and, being double glazed, an efficient barrier against those insidious winds.

The design of the house is a surprisingly sophisticated one, considering its basic cement block and steel frame construction. Such wide expanses of glass, together with a mezzanine, could be expected to make huge heating demands. In the beginning, under-floor heating was one of the options considered to cope with warming this large open space. But it was realised that a great deal of energy would be needed to heat the floor before inner space would be affected. The solution to the problem was finally quite simple. In the kitchen—which, incidentally, had ended up as a compact, enclosed area—a slow-combustion stove was installed. This does double duty: for cooking and heating. A small but effective electric pump forces heated water through two strategically placed, large-sized standard radiators in the living area. Since heat rises, the warmth is felt under the pitched roof in the mezzanine bedrooms where sliding wooden shutters let the heat in when they're open and keep the light out when they're closed.

Flooring also presented a problem. Tiling such a large area would have been costly, so a cement floor was chosen, this to be painted in a dark enough tone to absorb and conserve the sun's

heat. Here an unexpected problem arose when the contractor used the wrong type of sand and the floor developed a pattern of crazy-paving in modules almost the size of saucers. The whole job had to be done a second time.

The wide, open fireplace does stalwart duty during winter. Its early predisposition to smoke the place out was solved by the simple means of raising the firebed one brick level. In the cooler months a couch and chairs encircle the hearth, but in summer they are placed nearer the open windows.

A wide overhang above the wrap-around terrace simulates the classic Australian veranda. Walls of glass are designed as sliding panels that can be pushed back to leave only three of them stationary. Thus summer breezes from the river, which can be seen from every angle inside the house, keep the house cool on even the hottest day.

Both interior and exterior were painted in a soft ochre colour that blends with the natural clay of the surrounding terrain. A muted olive green, the colour of gumleaves, is used for contrast. It's a subtle and very suitable blend of colours that marries well with the bush environment.

There is only one enclosed living space in the house: the small, self-contained flat used by the owner's mother when she visits. Otherwise the house has a totally open plan. 'It's probably not the absolutely ideal solar energy house,' Lyndsay Pratt admits, 'that is, not an architect's design full of state-of-the-art technology, but it does just what we wanted it to do.' It is a house in tune with its surroundings, and its ambience, inside and out, makes for pleasantly relaxed living. 'Plan number seven' worked out to be modern, individual and energy efficient while paying homage to its country origins.

From the mezzanine bedrooms, when the sliding wooden shutters are opened, the entire living area below can be seen at a glance. The view beyond the windows is never obscured. Blinds and curtains weren't considered necessary, because the house has an absolutely private aspect from every side.

The handsome marmalade cat who has adopted the place obviously isn't insensible to the solar virtues of the house. Here he takes full advantage of afternoon sun as it warms the terrace.

142

*The area around the fireplace is the
unquestioned centre of activity during
the winter months. But when the sun
shines, it floods in; this warmth,
together with that of the judiciously
placed heaters, gives a boost to the
fire's heat. The William Morris print
on the linen covering the couch and
chairs is a splash of colour and
pattern, together with the Turkoman
rugs, to enliven this large open area.*

A local stonemason put in the new entrance steps and a low wall to surround the olive tree. New cladding boards, matching existing ones, soon rejuvenated the façade, and pale grey painted window boxes that bloom with colour have transformed the house.

Red-hued leaves fall into a birdbath surrounded by jonquils and azalea bushes. Water in a garden will always attract birds.

For all seasons

THIS little cottage under its canopy of trees must have been the fantasy of many an avid gardener in its time. It was built around the turn of the century, with two rubble and stucco chimneys to prove its age, as do the well-established old trees on the property. Its fortunes have waxed and waned. Six or so different families have grown up here.

From the 1930s until the 1970s it was the centre of an apple orchard. Across the dirt road, on the neighbouring property, strawberries were grown and then sent off to Sydney by train. It was a productive time, and the place must have been busy with fruit-pickers in the season.

The cottage, neatly positioned in the centre of its four hectares, was embellished with a garden to which each successive tenant made a contribution. One of the earliest owners was a sea captain who planted most of the bulbs that still, each year from June to August, raise their golden heads in celebration. While these daffodils and jonquils have endured, only a couple of the orchard trees are left. An old elm, a magnolia, willows and crab-apple trees are still there, and a grand, grey olive tree grows by the front door. Perhaps that too was the sea captain's doing, in memory of some Mediterranean voyage.

By the time the present owner bought the property it had become a 'renovator's dream', and most of the garden had disappeared under an enchanted forest of tangled vines. The house too was a mass of additions and subtractions, disguised and otherwise. Wall surfaces came in many kinds and colours, and the floor levels took a step up or down from one room to the next. It was in reality a renovator's nightmare. But Dawn Town is a gardener, and the traces of its past attractions were enough to win her over.

'To hide the dubious fibro walls and ceilings,' she says, 'pine panelling was the answer. Not only did it look sunny, but being an effective insulator it made the place cosy.' A couple of walls were removed; closing in a veranda enlarged one bedroom; putting in skylights lightened an erstwhile dark hall. So many alterations took place in the first couple of years, it was hard to keep count of them.

Among the most telling improvements were the installation of large windows, so the garden could be seen, and the opening up of a sunroom to extend the living room and give it a garden view as well. A local stonemason did a sterling job building a big open fireplace; after that he installed a flight of sandstone and slate steps to redesign the front entrance and built a raised stone bed to encircle the olive tree growing at the front door. Some wooden boards to match the earlier facing, a coat of white paint for the exterior, and grey wooden shutters painted to match the window boxes transformed the façade. Very soon it was hard to recognise the 'renovator's dream'.

Even in autumn the garden has life. Jonquils, planted by the sea captain who was one of the early owners of the property, spring to life as the deciduous trees begin to carpet the ground with their spent colour.

From the large windows which were installed so that the garden aspect could be enjoyed, the old olive tree can be seen. While having breakfast here it is possible to watch blue-black bowerbirds foraging with their dowdy, dull-green mates. Bird life in this garden offers a wide variety, from blue wrens in the fuchsia bushes to domestic geese around the dam on the hill.

An old pine chest with multiple brass locks is a handy catch-all beside a window that overlooks the shaded pool. This room once was a bedroom but has been opened up to extend living space.

The garden too has had some tender loving care. The old trees have been underplanted with azaleas, camellias and perennials. A ground cover of wild strawberries grows luxuriantly underfoot. In all, the garden area has been extended by a quarter-hectare. Sometimes a stray bloom appears, a reminder of the time when seeds and seedlings from this garden were a commercial proposition.

Today the property almost lives up to the legend hanging on a sign at the gate, 'Devon Farm'. It now has a population of three donkeys, two golden labradors, a marmalade cat and three geese, which were currently visiting a neighbouring property where they've discovered a few of their fine feathered friends. Old rambling roses are still blooming on fences and trellises, and the little cottage is growing old very gracefully.

A unique collection of antique kitchen utensils decorates the shelves of an old white kitchen dresser. It's hard to guess at the uses of some of these rare old pieces, but what is certain is that they were made to last a very long time. Each item is sturdy enough to survive years of use in family kitchens.

A CERTAIN STYLE

STYLE is a word that covers such a diversity of things that you suddenly realise its true meaning may actually be self-expression. Style is something we all have, though some of us have more of it than others. And when we say 'a certain style', we mean not only an individual look but one that is outstanding for its flair and distinction.

But, in the context of this book, how does a certain style mesh with country style, if each is so distinctive? Well, putting the two together isn't a problem; combining self-expression with a country look is really describing Australian country style to a T. For example, putting together things that are old and new, things that owe more to comfort than fashion, that have closer ties to history than to the shock of the new—that's what country style is

about. Having the assurance to be an innovator; to mix these items, to use strong or subtle colours as the situation requires, to prize old furniture that has certainly seen better days is also what it's about. Old things are the real basis of the country look, but adding a few striking newly created ones—that's where *style* comes in.

In choosing a house and decorating it, we take this self-expression to its fullest. But when we build or renovate a house on our own bit of land and furnish it with things we've gathered and stored over the years, that is unquestionably the essence of a certain style.

Shelves built into the wall beside the stairs leading to the guest mezzanine offered a clever solution to the housing of an extensive library. The little grey leather-covered chair belonged to David as a child; his father had it re-upholstered as a gift for his new grandson, Jock. When the clock was delivered, it posed a problem: where to put it? The space just beside the front door proved ideal. Set into the paving at the threshold is a foundation stone which came from one of the old Mort stores at Sydney's Darling Harbour.

150

At the front door, hydrangeas in terracotta pots revel in their shady spot. The entrance to the house is an unexpected foil to the otherwise plain sweep of unadorned side walls.

Shedding convention

WHEN seen from the road, across the paddocks and the dam, this house blends so effortlessly with its terrain that you catch only a glimpse of it as you pass by. But it's a house that really stands out as an innovative exercise in home building. It isn't an architect-designed award winner but an owner-built expression of individuality. Long ago, David Mort decided that his most pressing need in a house would be space. 'A normal house makes me claustrophobic,' he says. 'Perhaps the height of the ceilings has something to do with it.'

A building like this in the city would probably be called a warehouse. Such open space has become popular over the past decade or so in cities like New York and London. Here in the country, this building goes by the name of shed, your basic, corrugated-iron shed. But, what style it has.

Starting with a lean budget of twenty thousand dollars, David was able to pay for the bricks that form the floor, have the frame and roof erected, and have the power connected and a water tank installed. Then it was time for ironing out the wrinkles between cash flow and delivery of materials. Sheets of corrugated iron proved to be quite manageable modules for a lone builder to handle, and, over time, the building took shape.

For years David had been a collector of things. Among them were the cast-iron columns that now grace the brick-paved terrace facing the dam. 'It's a funny thing, but after I'd bought them, while I was still at school, I thought that I'd better do something to preserve them, so I gave them a coat of iron oxide to keep them from rusting. Then, after all that time, when I installed them here, the colour seemed so right to me that I left them just as they were.'

He has been most inventive in recycling and re-using materials. The louvred shutters for the french windows that open onto the terrace, for instance, were made by David from fence palings cut down the middle and attached to the frame. In the bathroom, brass piping, the kind used by plumbers, has been

fashioned into towel and shower rails. At one stage the interior walls were lined with hessian, but that has since been replaced by plasterboard. It's this fresh and lively element of making do, combined with the wonderfully stylish furnishings, that make this house unique.

David wrote about the house to his bride-to-be, Clarissa, who was teaching in England at the time. Her colleagues were astounded at the idea of having corrugated-iron walls and worried about how she'd hang the wallpaper. But it has never been a problem for Clarissa. She was even sorry to see the hessian go, especially from the bathroom, where it looked almost chic beside white porcelain.

The open plan of the house makes an airy and spacious gallery in which David and Clarissa's furnishings also have made a happy marriage. Their dining-room chairs are a perfect example. Half of them were hers and the other half his.

ABOVE LEFT
This marvellous bowl of full-blown roses conjures up images of days of wine and roses in Epernay. The area in which the house is built, being wine country too, has the kind of soil that produces wonderful roses as well as bountiful grape harvests.

LEFT
The jarrah dining table, designed and made by Simon Pockley, is vast and heavy. On the wall above it, a strong statement is made by the hanging created for David's aunt, Mary White, whose school of design influenced many young designers over the years.

A CERTAIN STYLE

ABOVE
In the sitting area a camel-back sofa awaits a choice of covering, though its white calico looks ideal. The sofa was made in Tasmania by James Bradley.

On the wall are two sets of six lovely botanical prints by Celia Rossen. One set was a gift from Clarissa's father; the other six prints were found at a Melbourne gallery. 'We were

incredibly lucky to find another signed set,' David says. The pine cupboard in the far corner holds a complete antique set of dessert plates, much used, the pattern worn, but charming.

OPPOSITE

The master bedroom has an atmosphere of rustic charm that is enhanced by its outlook to the rose garden. The rustic bedhead and bedside tables were made in Mudgee. On the wall by the window a painting by the late Sir Charles Lloyd Jones was a wedding gift to the Morts. An antique blanket chest offers fine storage space at the foot of the bed.

RIGHT

The bathroom also contains rustic furniture, so much at home with brick-paved floors. The old wire plant stand is usually festooned with greenery, but at this time of the year new plants had just been put in. Here, as throughout the entire house, one sees the sureness of touch that gives the house such élan.

BELOW

One of the attributes of corrugated iron is that it cools quickly at night. This bedroom certainly gives the impression of being a quiet, cool spot, and the view beyond the window enhances it.

Grouped together now, as they are, around the expansive refectory table designed by Simon Pockley, the chairs look as if they were carefully chosen to complement each other.

The Morts have put tremendous thought and effort into every aspect of this house, from the careful matching and reglazing of old french doors by David to Clarissa's idea for the bookshelves, built beside the stairs leading to the mezzanine guest room, which is so practical.

In building this house, these two have shrugged off convention to make their own personal statement. 'You put up with the imperfections; they're not important,' says David. And it's true that when you enter this house it's the pleasant ambience, the relaxed atmosphere and the assured sense of style you notice. The Morts have surrounded themselves with well-loved family things that maintain their ties with past generations.

This is the best of Australian country style—uncomplicated, easygoing and keenly attuned to the real and good things of life.

Near by, in the rose garden, an abundant show of blooms perfumes the air all season long. It makes the most wonderful cutting garden to fill the house with splendid bowls of roses.

A charming antique garden seat from Clarissa's family home has been set in place around a newly planted tree. In time, this will become one of the focal points of a garden that is just now beginning to take shape.

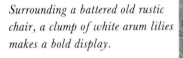

Surrounding a battered old rustic chair, a clump of white arum lilies makes a bold display.

OPPOSITE PAGE
On the front veranda, facing the green barrier that acts as a windbreak, the two twig chairs are, surprisingly, newly made. Behind them, one of the ancient camellias shows the last of its seasonal colour.

RIGHT
This exterior view shows the hexagonal conservatory which was added at one end of the veranda. On the far side, the cypress windbreak towers over the house, sheltering it.

The cream of country

IT is hard imagining how this old house, the homestead on a disused dairy property, must have looked just a few years ago. Even though the new owners have 'before' shots to show its past condition, it is an unbelievable transformation. But mostly it is a testimonial to the strength of imagination and the dedication of Susan and John Curtis, who share a single, uncompromising vision. And yet, while the changes they've wrought have been sweeping, the essential Australian character of the place has not been lost. Not only has this essence been retained, but now it seems dramatically enhanced.

This house, like many others of its era, was well positioned on the land, but the interior aspect was less than optimum. Its front doors and windows faced down the valley into the prevailing wind, which could be a murmuring breeze or a biting gale funnelling in from the ocean to the east. In fact, the reason for the dense windbreak hedge protecting the front door became evident almost as soon as the new owners had moved in their handyman kit. This wall of greenery had obviously served its purpose well, allowing several venerable, bloom-laden camellias to give years of pleasure to the house's occupants. 'Heaven knows how long they must have been there,' Susan comments, and a glance at their nobly entwined trunks testifies to a very ripe old age.

The most immediate need was to change and refocus the aspect of the house. So the entry, originally a narrow hall bisecting the cramped rooms on either side of it, was opened up to create a spacious dining room. Then, two more small rooms became one to make the living room. What was once the back door became the front entrance. It was a remarkable about-face that gave the house the roomy feel such a country place deserves to have.

The exterior of the house remained mostly unchanged, except

OPPOSITE
The subtle colour used for the interior is the perfect foil for old furniture whose wood is mellowed with age, as in the armoire shown here.

LEFT
Another angle of the living room shows an old meat-safe, now doing service as a wine cupboard. The chairs and sofa have been upholstered in a subtle near-match of plaid patterning. The rustic tree-fork table holds a lamp made from a wine jar still in its original wicker basket. A grain scoop and an iron candlestick decorate the chest.

for the addition of a hexagonal conservatory which adjoins both the kitchen and the living room. 'I'm not too sure about the shape of this room,' Susan comments. 'It's not in keeping with the general architecture. Still, it's a glorious place to sit in the sun.' Indeed, it gives a 270-degree vista of the gully, the hills, the silo, sheds and the newly installed tennis court up on the rise. The family being enthusiastic tennis players, the court was an early addition to the property. No swimming pool is on the

agenda, however. 'The beach is so close; we'd much prefer to go there,' Susan says.

The house was originally built in 1815. Later, in the early 1900s, Federation additions were tacked on. The pattern of its growth came to light as renovation began. 'We were so lucky to find a local builder who had a real feeling for the way we wanted things to be,' says Susan. This working relationship was remarkable for many things, but primarily for the speed with

which the whole undertaking was completed. Work was begun even before the contract was signed. They discovered convict-made bricks behind the fireplace, and old cedar from cupboards in one room was used for shelving in another. Altogether, everything possible was recycled and reused.

Throughout the house, coir matting has been used as the floor covering. Walls are painted in subtle variations of a parchment colour—the inspiration for this came from paint already on the walls of an original bedroom. For the wood mouldings a muted green was chosen. In the kitchen the floor was painted. It seems the painter needed some persuading to undertake this job. 'But the finished effect is just what we wanted,' Susan says. 'It's beginning to be a little scuffed, but I don't mind that.'

The whole renovation was carried out between September 1988 and February 1989, the result of immaculate co-ordination and boundless energy. 'We finished in time to celebrate my husband's birthday here,' Susan says, 'though the paint on the shelves wasn't dry and I was going around at the last minute using the hair dryer on the last tacky bits.'

OPPOSITE
The conservatory is a showplace for the Curtises' wonderful collection of Australiana. In the centre of the room an old chest holds a modern iron candlestick as well as an old oil lamp and an elegantly carved old wooden bowl. A Jimmy Possum chair sits against the window, beyond which the green countryside can be seen. Little is known of the elusive bush carpenter Jimmy Possum, but his work is recognised from the ingenious design that dispensed with stretchers yet was strengthened by the weight of a person sitting in the chair.

RIGHT
Through another window the barbecue area with its rustic furniture, the tennis court and, beyond it, the silo and outbuildings can be seen.

RIGHT
Beside the fireplace, built of old convict bricks, modern wrought-iron fire tongs look very much at home.

This house has style, veritable Australian country style, not only because of its intrinsic character but equally because of the remarkable collection of authentic old pieces that furnish it. As well, there's a certain urbanity that just hints at Susan's admiration for Ralph Lauren's design concepts. It's altogether a wonderful blend of the old and the new. While the couch and chairs in the living room are new, they have the pleasantly muted look of long-used things. Susan had them covered in plaid upholstery fabrics made by Robert Allen. 'I wanted them to look as if they'd always been there,' she says.

OPPOSITE
In the dining room a modern metal chandelier with the ornate design of an earlier era is perfectly at home with a fine old English oak table and chairs. A charming little rocking horse of early Australian design sits close by. The handsome quilt used as a wall hanging is American. Though this room's furnishing is eclectic, everything is in perfect balance.

One can only marvel at the fine examples of old Australiana that Susan and John have collected to furnish their refuge from the modern world. 'We have a network of places where we know we'll find what we're looking for,' Susan says. Her list of sources is surprisingly long and scattered around the country. Their choices have been catholic. 'Our criterion is that things that are old should look old,' Susan explains.

Now that the house is complete, the next project will be to improve the surrounding landscape. Having run dairy cattle, the land is somewhat barren of trees and foliage. 'I've discover-

OPPOSITE AND RIGHT
Carefully selected old pieces like the the three-cornered stick chair in the living room and the rustic gate in the entrance hall have a sculptural simplicity that makes them so much greater than the sum of their parts. Even the simple iron hand tools and rakes have new life here.

LEFT AND OPPOSITE
The bedrooms have a simple elegance which comes from the sure way furnishing fabrics and colour have been used. The basic nature of coir matting and white cotton canvas gives these rooms character that is integral to the country theme. With the addition of old quilts as wall hangings, pine and oak furniture enhanced with the patina of age, there is a restful atmosphere that more modern rooms can rarely give.

ed there's a very good gardener living locally, we're already discussing plans for a walled garden,' Susan says. 'And we have a big tree-growing scheme for next year.' With so much land at her disposal, the result should be impressive. There's to be a lake below the house which will probably be the focus of the landscape design.

And after that, what? Susan confesses to being an inveterate collector. 'I've never parted with anything,' she says. 'Never, never, never.' So there will have to be another project.

COUNTRY LIVING IN THE CITY

IN the hustle and bustle of city life, most of us just go with the flow. We've got the measure of the pace. Our eyes are attuned to modern décor as we see it in offices, shops and increasingly in today's popular restaurants. The hard-edge look is city style. So it's no surprise that we find these trends in our private living quarters too.

But there's a great deal to be said for having a totally different home environment from the one we encounter in the outside world. If a change is really as good as a holiday, then a holiday feeling might easily be had simply by changing the ambience in which we live.

We found proof of this in the houses you'll see in this chapter. From the outside they look exactly like their terrace neighbours. But on the inside all resemblance ends. Here you find the simplicity and comfort that can transport you, in imagination, to open country. Here, the owners' lovingly collected old furniture and hand-crafted bric-à-brac make a mellow, uncontrived setting.

This restful feeling is perhaps the strongest characteristic of country style. Nothing in it seems to confront or challenge you. There's no need for kid-glove handling as there is with contemporary furnishing. You'll find that nice old things that are weathered and used don't put the constraints of custodianship upon you. They make no demands for constant polishing and cosseting; they're easygoing, easy to live with.

Country style is truly the most relaxed way to furnish a house. And when you have to contend with the stress of city living, that's like being on holiday in your own home.

On the hand-braided rug, this sturdy old blanket chest, scarred with much travel and use, holds an ornately decorated wooden storage box. A simple earthenware bowl, typical of country and peasant pottery, is decorated with a bold brushed design. An object lesson in grouping disparate old things in country style, this is an attractive and distinctive display.

In the dining area, a splendid Amish quilt, in typically muted tones, is a strong motif against white walls. On the weathered pine table a papier mâché basket from Tasmania holds rolls; handmade glasses hold the wine; and a unique old whirlygig in carved wood, from Bendigo, circa 1890, gives an authentic country twist. Mismatched chairs of wicker and wood, with old hand-hooked seat cushions, give a soft homey air.

Collector's cache

SOME people are obsessive about collecting things, and their search takes them far afield. Dense jungles and deep seas hold no fears for the seeker of the rare cymbidium or endangered crustacean. But Trish Hurst's collecting passion is for things that enhance her home as well as gladden her heart. When she returns from her quests she brings to her showplace home spoils of a gently domesticated kind that decorate and delight. Trish is a collector of country things.

It all began for her in 1976 when she left her job with *Vogue* magazine and, with her husband and baby son, Chris, who was just eight months old at the time, set out for an extended visit to America. They organised a motor home and 'just took off'. It turned into a nine-month adventure in which they visited thirty-two states. During that time she bought her first quilt and her first decoy duck. The collecting bug had bitten.

'After that, one summer in New York, I invested in my first collection,' she says. 'Quilts have been my specialty ever since.' Though they would remain her first love, her country collection has certainly diversified widely since then. Now, though she may go to New York once or twice a year to develop her collection, sometimes trading back certain things and buying others, Australiana plays an ever-increasing part in her acquisition of country treasure. 'But it will become increasingly rare and hard to find,' she predicts.

To visit her small semi-detached cottage is to discover the most delightful cache of hand-carved, stitched and crafted objects, each one with a wonderful story to tell. And Trish tells their story well. Her knowledge of country things and their derivation is encyclopaedic. Being a purist, she makes sure the provenance of everything in her collection is minutely catalogued. In fact, collecting old wares and artefacts comes close to being a conservationist's crusade with her.

Of her fellow country enthusiasts she says with a smile, 'We're not the ones who are felling the forests so people can have new furniture.' Of course she's right; collectors of old things are dedicated exponents of recycling, because they rediscover artisan-made things and give them new utility.

When Trish found her present house, one of the first things she did was sand back the floorboards and give them a coat of beeswax. This base of simple honest wood immediately set the scene for the casual look her country things demanded. It's the perfect foil for the muted colours of the old country furniture and bibelots. The sharp contrast of stark white walls throws everything into relief, giving every object definition as the eye moves from one treasure to another. Beyond her living room window, a long-established giant white gum sets a country scene for her in the middle of the city.

In the bedroom, filtered light through moveable shutters makes the right mellow mood for the old quilts that cover the bed and bedside table and make a gentle note as a wall hanging; this one a youth quilt, probably made for an old trundle bed. Two Old Order Amish dolls, faceless and featureless, rest on European pillowslips embellished with handmade Victorian lace. Bare floorboards offer an ideal background for braided rugs.

A stencilled lid gives a subtle decorative touch to this expertly carved pine box. On the lamp table the lamp base is an old Australian bung jar; the shade's cover is a softly toned checked fabric that picks up the pattern used to cover the couch. The carved yacht is a skilful example of well-scaled replication in materials that echo the original object.

On top of the old meat-safe, a small carving in the round of two robin redbreasts accompanies a single moveable figure carved in wood with a black face on one side and a white one on the other—discrimination according to how the wind blew. A wooden deed box with two compartments and brass fittings completes the display.

Quiet achievement

SOMETIMES fashion dictates our enthusiasms. Not so in the case of this house. Its furnishing is the result of simple dedication that has lasted for a decade or more. Unconcerned with decorating trends, Ruth Turnell has always loved the character of old things. The look and feel of old country pieces have been her fancy since she was a student in Queensland.

Each of Ruth's acquisitions has a special meaning for her, either from its remembered source or its cost. As a student with limited funds, she found that every treasure meant some sacrifice, large or small. But now that these things have found their place in her inner-city house, it is their contribution to her peace of mind that gives them new value for her. With her busy schedule as a teacher, working toward her master's degree, she finds the easy ambience of her country furnishings adds to her sense that this house is her haven.

Despite the many demands of her professional life and the maintenance of her house, she musters the energy to indulge in another of her interests. Quilting is the ideal handicraft for someone with a love of country style. Her projects, even while still in work, add colour and character to her home. Stretched on frames, they make attractive splashes of colour to decorate the rooms, wherever she may be working on them at the time.

Ruth has the instinct of a collector. No matter where you look in her small house, you'll find things of interest and curiosity. Open a cupboard; there's pottery and glass, old, antique or craftsman made. Open the drawer of an old cedar chiffonier and see stacks of old lace and linen folded away. 'My mother's always finding things for me,' Ruth says. So, it runs in the family.

The old pine dresser dates from the late 1800s. The 'Rose' soup tureen was bought in an outback town and the remainder of the dinner service was bought in Gympie, so even though they are modern they do have country connections.

This very old meat-safe once served as the pantry in Ruth's kitchen. Now it is elevated to holding her collection of china and glass. On top she keeps her cookbooks, an old stoneware bread crock, Italian blue stipple bowls and a reproduction oil lamp.

ABOVE

Sitting on top of an old wooden blanket chest is one of Ruth's most prized possessions; made and decorated by her grandfather before she was born, this book-box holds some sentimental memorabilia.

LEFT

In the dining room an old wooden dogcart, made for Mormon children in Utah, gives a touch of family life to a window nook. This grouping enlivens an enclosed corner of the inner-city terrace house.

OPPOSITE

The dining table is an old government-issue writing desk; the bentwood and stamped-back chairs are also old. Flannel flowers always look lovely, and the blue glazed jug and stipple bowl complement them perfectly.

Terrace incognito

THIS house is flanked on either side by a whole block of similar inner-city terrace houses. But its anonymous exterior conceals its true character, for there are two things about it that distinguish it from the other houses. Firstly, it has a garden that could almost qualify as rainforest. In size it is no more than an average terrace backyard; after that there is no comparison. This garden is dappled with green-filtered light, screened through the leaves of a massive Port Jackson fig. Vines tangle over the lattice fences; ferns and shrubs run riot under the canopy of leaves above them. It is in itself a green mansion.

The second distinguishing factor is that, inside, the owner has collected a wealth of wonderful old pieces with which to furnish it. Her discerning eye has not restricted her choice to any one period or style. In fact, the collection is nothing if not

OPPOSITE PAGE
A bentwood and cane chaise longue, an original from the Viennese furniture maker Thonet (who at the turn of the century revolutionised seating with the innovation of bentwood), and another of his pieces, a desk chair, give a country look in a room with a fine old Kelim rug on its floor.

BELOW
A triptych mirror, sparely framed, reflects the stairs and the french doors, making a small space seem larger. A fine collection of moulded glass from the last century, by its transparency, does not destroy the illusion of space as it stands on a cantilevered marble mantel in this narrow room.

183

A French carved silver gilt mirror reflects a collection of Georgian glass, and a Max Dupain photograph of a peace lily hangs beside a potted one in the jardiniere.

There's a romantic, old-world charm to this bedroom, with its modern lace-trimmed mosquito net made in Fiji. During the day the net is drawn up in graceful swags, tied with white satin ribbon. The net itself is cleverly attached to the ceiling, again with ribbons tied to eyelet hooks. Additional lace for the lower edge 'cost more than the net itself', its owner says. The

Victorian towel stand displays old-fashioned lace, and the potpourri bowl by the bed is the delicate 'Spring' pattern by Wilkinson.

COUNTRY LIVING IN THE CITY

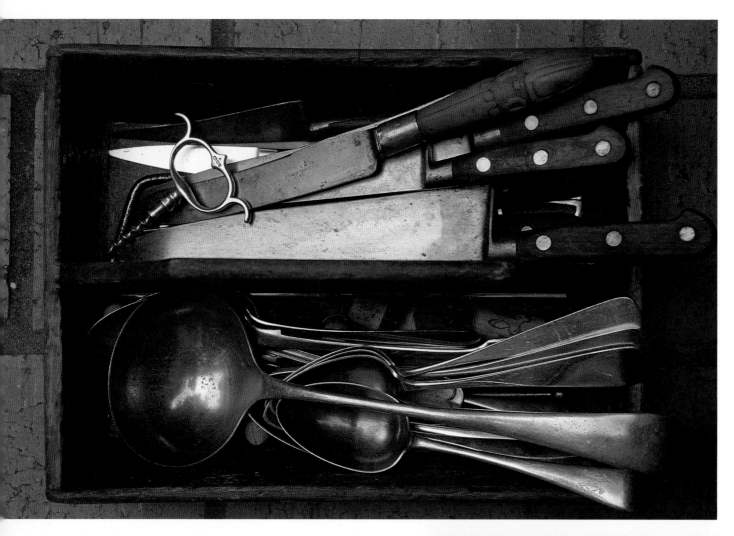

An old wooden cutlery tray holds a
collection of antique silver on one side
and well-used old kitchen knives on the
other. Such trays are back in use.

A big terracotta jug is an attractive
receptacle for an array of wooden
kitchen implements, while the old wire
baskets keep ingredients close at hand
for the cook on a serviceable modern
benchtop. Old and new mix well.

On the scrubbed Huon pine chiffonier a collection of interesting nineteenth-century storage pots and bowls are assembled. The salt-glazed pot at left once had a wooden lid; the turquoise copper-glazed pot with small handles once stored potted meat or oil. The tall Barr candlesticks are white porcelain.

eclectic, but with a tendency toward certain old country pieces. These objects are among the best examples of their kind.

When an architect was called in to help with planned renovations, interior space was opened up to accommodate the collection. After all, small terrace houses are generally on a scale to take only the most necessary furnishings. But there is more to manipulating space than knocking down walls; with her choice of subtle colours and simplified structure, the owner has made a setting that shows off her collection to advantage.

OPPOSITE

*Long admired as it stood on the
veranda of a country house out west,
this antique hand-crafted potplant
stand at last changed hands when its
new owner, seeing it rusting away,
offered to buy it. Since then it has been
sanded back and painted to preserve it
for many more years.*

RIGHT

*A handmade terracotta birdbath nestles
among bird's-nest ferns beside a trellis.
A birdbath, the owner says, is an
essential ingredient in a garden for
anyone wanting to attract birdlife.*

A cosy confederation

BUILT in 1926 on land that had been subdivided early in 1920, this house was erected over a track that once had led from Vaucluse House, in Sydney, to its chapel. Its owner, John Williams, was attracted to the house at first sight. 'The thing that sold it to me were the built-in window boxes,' he says. But it must have been more than that, for the house has many attributes. A sandstone foundation, jarrah floors, beamed ceilings and interior leadlight sliding doors all must have contributed to his making a decision to buy it.

And of course, the garden. There was a small surprise in store for John regarding this. 'One day,' he says, 'a chap arrived at the door and said, "I harvest your seeds every year."' So John agreed that he could go into the garden. After a while, the visitor, who turned out to be a seed merchant, came to the door with chequebook in hand saying apologetically that he could pay only six hundred dollars this year because the yield of Kentia palm seeds wasn't as high as usual. 'It was then I realised that the garden was income earning,' John says, 'and I put the money into my garden improvement fund at once.'

Because John is an antique dealer, he has always been able to furnish his house with the things he most admired. And because it is quite a big house with a number of rooms, it's possible to select the things whose colour enhances the setting: a *sang-de-boeuf* bowl where red looks best, or celadon or blue-and-white porcelains grouped together according to their colour.

Pre-luncheon drinks are served in the shade of fine old trees. The marble-topped table that matches the cast-iron and wood chairs is perfect in this garden setting.

On the front balcony of a fine Federation house, morning tea is set out on a hand-embroidered teacloth that matches the 1920s teaset. The silver teapot is Georgian. The matching wicker chairs and table, circa 1930, are quite rare finds.

LEFT
Oriental ceramics adorn this window setting. The large vase is Arita; the green glazed pot is nineteenth-century French. The pretty sofa is covered in a fresh floral-printed linen that complements the ceramic colours.

OPPOSITE
A superb collection of Georgian and Victorian crystal is displayed on a window sill. An unusual pair of ship's decanters are engraved 'OUTWARD BOUND' and 'HOMEWARD BOUND'.

This Federation house in its lovely garden once had 'quite a nice little view', John says, but this unfortunately has been built out and only a glimpse remains. But what isn't lost is the essential character of a house that has hardly been changed in over sixty years.

COUNTRY LIVING IN THE CITY

OPPOSITE

The furniture in this Federation bedroom was made expressly for it in the 1940s. The picture frame is made of the same wood as the bedhead and wardrobe; the wall frieze was painted to match the fabric chosen for the bed.

This beautiful wooden bed was once owned by Ezra Norton, publisher of the Truth *newspaper. It was made in France and decorated with ormolu motifs. Note the picture frame on the bedside table, a splendid example of silver-plate art nouveau.*

Spring flowers bloom as border plantings in a garden plan that was devised to reflect the Federation character of the house. The urns were made at the turn of the century.

A good garden should always have an air of mystery, as this one certainly does. Sandstone paths lead through dense foliage, a veritable forest of camellias, ferns and palms.

Wollombi House has been restored to its former simple glory. The way it looks today is the result of a massive amount of research and renovation. The original roof was a single gable, however, changed to the one seen here somewhere along the line.

HAVENS

GETTING away from it all has more appeal today than ever before. There are so many reasons to leave the city behind and head for the hills. Country living is the reverse side of the modern coin, and if you can occasionally spend some time away from it all, it's an investment in peace of mind. The confrontations of the city—pollution, noise, the need to rush, the urge to succeed—all leave us gasping for that proverbial breath of fresh air that only the country can give us.

Unfortunately, most of us can't effect the change from city pressure to country peace whenever we'd like. But still, this ideal of escaping is something we cling to. Though most of us are city dwellers, with few actual ties to country life, we all know the value of a spell away. There are, however, some dedicated souls who have managed to make the break, either on a long-term basis or regularly for short therapeutic visits. In this chapter we find three very different answers to making a haven away from it all. Though they are all different, they do have a common denominator—bucolic bliss.

Mind you, none of them was easily come by. Each one demanded a high degree of effort from its owner. So much so that most of us would probably have jibbed at it. But what a reward for their labours for these happy few who have their own bit of country to escape to!

If the prospect of so much hard work is enough to daunt you, take heart. For you there are places like Wollombi House that offer you the chance to spend a weekend, or longer if you choose, as a guest. On such a visit you could share vicariously in the rewards of having a haven away from it all.

Old-fashioned flowers surround the front steps behind which the ironbark piers and bearers have all been repaired and restored.

199

A rarely used door into the kitchen has been curtained with lace panels. Though they look as if they might be quite special, Evelyn affirms that they are in fact easily found.

Love in bloom

THIS is a love story. It is a simple, straightforward affair with a happy ending. When the present owner first saw this house years ago, it was love at first sight. She had spent holidays and weekends at her little cottage in the town and knew the area well. When Wollombi House was put up for sale in 1985, she knew the time had come to declare her intentions.

She quit her job with the National Trust, sold her cottage and everything else to move into her dream home. But at that time it was closer to Cold Comfort Farm than to a rose-covered cottage. Even so, this was the kind of challenge to fire Evelyn Bloom's imagination.

But it took more than imagination to set this house in order. Evelyn became a sleuth in a quest for the clues that would help her solve the puzzle of how Wollombi House looked in its heyday. And Miss Marple herself couldn't have done it better.

Evelyn had made the decision to renovate the house to a particular period in its history: to a time when it was at its best as a family home. The house was built in the early 1870s on ironbark piers, with a wrap-around veranda and a single-pitched roof. Set on a hill, it overlooked the Great North Road, which was then a busy conduit for produce from local farms and coal from the Maitland area of New South Wales.

The period that had taken Evelyn's interest was that from 1890 to 1940, when the family of Dr Albert Lee Bapty lived in the house. The doctor came from England, the youngest in a family of twelve boys. He was a very handsome, well-educated man who took up practice in what was then the declining town of Wollombi. Rust had ruined the local wheat crops, and the economy had flagged.

Dr Bapty set up his consulting room in the house, in a panelled room off the back veranda. A lattice divider was made to screen the family area from the patients who sat on benches, with a nice view of the valley before them, as they waited their turn. Mrs Bapty kept pretty much to herself while maintaining her well-appointed home.

To learn more about the previous tenants of her house, Evelyn Bloom went to Wolfhaven in Tasmania to talk to the last surviving Bapty daughter, Irene, who was then in her nineties. She could still remember much about Wollombi House during her family's tenure.

At the bathroom window a pretty collection of blue-and-white ceramic pieces hint at the charming character of the interior. The bathroom is carefully appointed, in character with its past, with washstands and an old-fashioned footed iron bath, but the plumbing is reassuringly modern.

This vista from the front door overlooks the barbecue area set up beside the native bush garden, which Evelyn has planted but doesn't believe in cultivating. Her philosophy for native plants is 'the survival of the fittest', and it seems to work.

201

Just as much research has gone into re-establishing the old-fashioned garden as into renovating the house itself. Here, statice—or sea lavender, as it's sometimes called—makes a healthy show beneath the nodding heads of an old-fashioned multiflora rose in bloom.

So, the jigsaw pieces gradually fell into place. All that was needed then was a massive amount of elbow grease from the owner to renovate the house and re-establish the old-fashioned garden plants. Luckily for Evelyn, she was no mean exponent of do-it-yourself home renovation. Years as a student in all kinds of courses began to pay off. She knew a lot about restoring antique furniture and, having set up her workshop in the garden shed on a rise above the house, got to work in earnest. Apart from specialist areas like electrical wiring and plumbing and restoring the heavy timber piers, the whole undertaking was a single-handed effort.

Having worked in the landscape section of the National Trust, she was also well equipped to tackle the garden renovation, particularly since gardens of the nineteenth century are her special interest. 'I never travel without a trowel and a plastic bag in the boot of the car,' she says. Many of her greatest finds have been plants discovered growing by the roadside or in churchyards. The garden now has lovely old roses and perennials that look as if they had always been there. In the natural bush area beyond the fence, her sure hand with native plants is also showing wonderful results.

Now that all the groundwork has been done and Wollombi House is so perfectly restored, Evelyn offers visitors the chance to enjoy the pleasures of country living. Her small business is thriving, with guests from overseas as well as local ones, some becoming regulars. It's easy to see why. Staying here is like reliving the days when Christmas was spent in the country with the family and the memory of it kept you going all year long.

The front veranda's worn and weathered timbers have supported many visitors. The old squatter's chairs and benches are always inviting. Inside the wicker basket, Evelyn Bloom keeps a treasure-trove of toys for visiting children. 'I never tell them what's there; I just let them discover it for themselves. Children are so curious about things. It doesn't take long for them to peek in to see what's inside.'

The cool hallway bisects the house so that from its shadowed depths you look through either the front door or the back door. During her research, Evelyn was told by someone who had known the house in early days that the hall's floor felt smooth and cool underfoot. From this she deduced that the floor covering must have been linoleum.

Black and white squares with a black
border was her choice for the linoleum
that was made to her order to cover the
floor hall. Blue stippled walls and the
handsome cedar joinery, milled from
local wood, give the house its
integrated character.

HAVENS

The Blue Bedroom is a particular
favourite with visitors. It is pretty and
peaceful—except perhaps at night
when the local wombat can be heard on
his nightly rounds.

RIGHT
The windows have been curtained with
charming swags of lace. This creates a
particularly soft and tranquil mood in
the bedrooms.

HAVENS

Purpose built

SET among great lichened boulders of seemingly primordial age, shaded by remarkably old wattle trees, this house itself might be any age at all. In fact, it's almost new. It came into being quite recently from its owners' discerning plan and was built as a hands-on experience. Carol and Tony Orford knew exactly what they wanted from a bush hide-away. Made to measure for and by them, it now rewards them generously for their labours.

Although it is new, in this well-weathered setting its appearance is mellow and the actual fabric of the house is bush-worn. Reused and recycled materials are what give it an honest, crafted-in-the-bush character.

The house sits on two hundred hectares of boulder-strewn hilly bush country, literally untameable in its wild beauty. That's why the Orfords love it. The feeling that man's hand has barely touched it enhances this paradise, where wallabies come down to the stream to drink and wild ducks nest under the sandy banks. Bellbirds call from unseen depths of scrub. It's a place apart, a far cry from the bustle and noise of cities like Sydney and London in which the Orfords spend their working life, frequently travelling between the two.

This place is their retreat, loved and respected by them. Though they understand the need to lay hands lightly on this land, they do enjoy the challenge of a certain careful husbandry. But they interfere sparingly with their bush domain. For instance, after a recent flood, when the stream broke its banks, uprooting young volunteer trees, they took great pains to replace the lost vegetation by replanting. A small vegetable patch has been their single intrusion into the wilderness—and that's no easy thing to maintain, with incursions by the occasional kangaroo foraging for supper.

If there is one problem in paradise, it is the invading flocks of feral goats, progeny of those let loose by farmers who, tiring of angora culture, left their remaining animals to forage for themselves. Their numbers have grown into sizeable, destructive groups. It is hoped they will be removed before they destabilise the native fauna's habitat. 'Tony's already doing battle,' Carol says with some satisfaction.

While the terrain is left as close to natural as possible and everything seems so little tampered with, a great deal of planning still went into the creation of this idyllic hideaway. The

The bush-made music stand was Tony Orford's own creation; in the true tradition of old-time bush carpenters he made it from twigs. The old table and chair give a place for quiet reading or writing or setting out the afternoon tea. Near by a simply made barbecue is available for the impromptu meal out of doors. It's the casual way of life and the slow tempo that makes this place such a perfect haven.

The house shelters under gumtrees, and tall old wattles are the backdrop. Veranda living is for summer pastimes: reading, snoozing in the hammock, writing letters, playing music, eating al fresco. On the hottest summer nights, sleeping out on the veranda is an alternative to a hot and restless night indoors. The veranda's role is a starring one all year long; when it's raining, life goes on busily under its sheltering overhang.

A decorated and studded old chest offers an ideal resting place for a basket of native flowers.

The open living area has the sitting room at one end and the kitchen, with a wood-burning stove and a commodious old table, at the other. Rustic and long-used pieces of furniture give a restful, unfussy air to the place. Life here is very much an indoor/outdoor arrangement.

house sits on a gentle rise under the lee of the surrounding hills. Below it the stream forms a wide pool. It was built on the spot from which the huge boulders on the hill opposite could be viewed and reflections in the water are most beautiful. The structure, with its bleached and weathered wood, is so in sympathy with the surroundings that it has become a natural part of the scene. The native animals pass by almost unaware that they are sharing their bush sanctuary.

RIGHT
*In the attic bedroom, old memorabilia
from India and the Far East add
interest to a simple rustic kind of room.*

LEFT
*Framed in the window, this weathered
chest of drawers with its peeling,
flaking paint has a colour that is muted
by age. On its sanded wooden top a
generous basket of dried and
everlasting flowers gives the easy touch
of colour that enlivens the room.*

OPPOSITE
*Outside, on the veranda wall,
a rustic coat-rack holds a decorative
wreath whose naive motif might be a
ferret and a fowl, or is it a cat and a
cock? Whatever the artist wanted to
depict, the result is charming; a lively
example of the bush artist's work and
something to be enjoyed in this ideal
setting, far away from machine-made,
hard-edged modern things of today.*

Upstairs in the attic bedroom, the ubiquitous mosquito net makes a decorative swag above the bed. The quilt, a gift from one of the Orfords' daughters, was planned to be hand quilted, but time ran out and it had to be machine-stitched in order to make Carol's birthday presentation on time.

This is a variation on the theme of teddy bear collections. Koalas make up the entire complement of this one, and they come in many shapes and sizes. Being natives, they're right at home in this bush house. Unfortunately the real live thing isn't indigenous to the area, but these are attractive stand-ins.

Away from it all

WHEN one's working life is demanding, creative and involved with the strenuous team effort of movie making, it isn't surprising that solitude gets high priority on the list of personal needs. The desire to opt out and enjoy the simple life, even for short periods, was the reason this slab hut was built by one such busy person. Its owner is a young woman in her early twenties, so it's all the more remarkable that she chose such a secluded patch of bush and asked a friend to help her build a simple hut. But her love of solitude leads her to spend as much of her precious leisure time as possible in a no-frills kind of living.

The hut has none of your modern conveniences. In a way, it is the next best thing to camping out, except that there's a

comforting air of permanence in having a roof over your head, an open fireplace, and a big old iron bedstead, quilt-covered and cosy, for times when the rain is beating a tattoo on the tin roof overhead. When a friend comes to spend the weekend, there's a snug wooden wagon to be used as a sleep-out. The bathhouse is roughly midway between it and the hut, with a water tank to keep it well supplied.

Some of the furnishings are props from film sets; the wagon for one, and a kerosene-tin chest of drawers for another. It's pretty much a case of life imitating art, and these acquisitions recall a time when making do was how most people got by.

There's an open fire for cooking on and keeping warm at in the winter. Old oriental rugs are scattered over the tamped-down earthen floor, adding the colour of a nomad's tent to the hut. There's altogether a great sense of escapism here, as if one had happened upon a carefree gypsy's camp.

A dam has been excavated near by, so summers too will soon be more relaxed with a swimming hole in which to cool off. Could there be a more relaxed haven? This surely is the ulti-mate place for a carefree retreat.

COUNTRY ORIGINS

A large white ceramic platter, thrown and decorated by Arthur Boyd. The Boyd family has a long connection with pottery making in Australia.

GETTING back to origins may sometimes mean taking a circuitous track and may even necessitate looking at things through the eyes of uncomprehending strangers of early days. Take, for example, the Kanguroo and Tigar mug in the Australian National Gallery. The inspiration for its design takes some tracing. From the kangaroo skins brought back by the botanist Joseph Banks from his voyage with Cook in 1768–71, the famous animal and sporting painter George Stubbs did a painting which he called *Kongouro of New Holland*. Later, in 1790, a wood engraving of a kangaroo, similarly posed, was published in London. Three years after that, the Kanguroo and Tigar mug was produced by a Staffordshire pottery. Today the last remaining original mug has found its way to the gallery in Canberra.

A more direct line leads back to the beginning of our most enduring country pottery. It was a disillusioned prospector, George Duncan Guthrie, who first set up the now famous pottery in Bendigo. The gold rush hadn't made everyone rich, and those who were smart turned their hand to other things. The fine clay from which so much alluvial gold had been wrested was still a rich lode for someone who understood its worth. By 1851 Guthrie had three large beehive kilns producing the sturdy, high-fired pottery that today still bears the Bendigo name and continues to thrive.

PERHAPS some of the most evocative pottery of more recent times is that of Merric Boyd. This studio potter worked in Melbourne for forty years. Though the impact of his work was not far reaching, his very personal expression had an exuberance that was entirely Australian in theme. His inimitable handmade pieces celebrate antipodean forms: gumnuts, leaves, tree trunks as well as native animals, all glazed in earthy country colours.

Pottery, by its impervious nature, outlasts many other materials, and even if it does get broken, the shards remain to tell the story. But we have been fortunate in husbanding our ceramics well, from the salt-glazed Bendigo ware which was produced along English lines but transposed easily, to the work of studio potters like Merric Boyd, his sons, and many others. And of course we also have access to all the imported pieces which, by virtue of a long connection, have earned their right to full citizenship and a place in our country-style houses.

OPPOSITE
Merric Boyd, who was a studio potter for more than forty years, created these intrinsically Australian themes for hand-coiled ceramic pieces.

RIGHT
Merric Boyd's favoured things from the Australian bush—gumnuts, leaves, and tree trunks, as well as native fauna—are all seen in his pottery.

The brown jugs here are from Bendigo Pottery. The butter churn is from Gisborne, Victoria, and other pieces are nineteenth-century French provincial in origin.

This collection of salt-glazed ceramic pitchers was started only five years ago, but already it is outstanding. There are many Ridgway and some Minton examples, and they vary from the delicate and intricately patterned to bolder replicas of corn on the cob and leaf-pattern shapes.

Old quilts, braided rugs and other early textiles may be harder to find, but they are no less exciting. The sad fact is that the ravages of time, and moth, take a heavier toll on these, so when you do have the good fortune to come upon some fine example of a hand-stitched or handmade piece, try to acquire it. And if you do, respect and care for it as it deserves.

Well-aged glass too, even of the most basic domestic kind, can also open up a window on history. For collectors, this is an area that has not yet become overpriced in the marketplace, which gives it added appeal. But sophisticated Georgian pieces are another matter; they are costly, but very beautiful, and worth making a sacrifice to own.

Silver made by early silversmiths in Australia has a certain rarity value, for the volume of such things was quite small. It is consequently to be prized both for its rareness and for its sometimes idiosyncratic uses and motifs, such as mountings for emu eggs and designs of leaping kangaroos.

Wine-jar lamp base, carved wooden bowl and an old salt-glazed jug holding native greenery have all the earmarks of country origins.

COUNTRY ORIGINS

RIGHT
This doll's dress and matching drawers were stitched in 1892 by Ethel Saywell, a student of Albion Street Public School in Sydney during Queen Victoria's reign.

OPPOSITE PAGE
A hand-stitched child's dress, circa 1890, is delicately gathered and tucked with lace inserts and edging and picked-thread work. From the hand of the dedicated Ethel Saywell, who must have been a prize pupil and very industrious indeed.

BELOW
A lovely example of the demanding stitchery that goes into producing such hand-crafted bags as this.

But it is in the area of the domestic arts and crafts that country style really turns back to its origins. From pieces of fabric stitched by some anonymous seamstress into charming samplers or garments to quilts and cushions lovingly embroidered, there is great variety of choice if you know where to look for them.

This urge to possess such scraps of history is growing because of the resurgence and appreciation of Australian country style. This is a trend that has nothing to do with the trendy. It is prompted by the desire to feel closer to our origins, and this movement has never been stronger than it is today. We are very much aware that conservation and the simple needs of country style go hand in hand. It is not too late for us to seek out and save our country origins.

Some fine stitchery went into this needlework piece depicting wattle on a gold and black ground.

'Ingenuity played a large part in the making of these one-off pieces. Some, of course, were strangely shaped indeed'

This framed sampler, stitched some twenty years ago, will almost certainly become a cherished heirloom in time.

ABOVE
*An attractive collection of antique
spoons and ladles, together with a
crystal perfume bottle, grace the top of
a small antique chest of drawers.*

ABOVE

An enamelled box and pencil case, both excellent examples from an era when craftsmanship was highly prized.

LEFT

A glass tumbler engraved with flannel flowers was typical of things that reflected the nationalist fervour of the years following Federation. This was made in 1912 and is prized today.

A collection of blue and green glass bottles decorate a window ledge. They are typical of the discoveries that collectors delight in making.

An old kerosene lamp with its glass shade sits in the window of a slab hut that sometimes has an overnight guest and therefore needs light.

Bottles like these often come to light on the sites of old or restored houses. These came from beneath the floorboards of their owner's renovated house. The slender one with the barley-sugar-twist neck once held sauce. The squat one with the lopsided top carries the legend 'Bumsted & Co, Table Salt'. Another once held lemonade. All are collector's items.

THE REAL STUFF

THE country furniture of every continent has its own particular style. In Europe, centuries of evolution and the flow of fashion have diluted national characteristics to a greater or lesser degree. But in countries like America and Australia, much shorter histories have left their colonial idioms more or less intact.

The colonists of America often had the advantage of group settlement, and their artefacts and furniture reflect this civilising effect with more ornate, often decorated surfaces—the Pennsylvania Dutch or Hispanic traditions, for example, or the immaculately crafted furnishings that were starkly simple in the Shaker and Amish manner. But in Australia the furniture made for country dwellings, for isolated slab huts or workmanlike station homesteads, were of necessity plain and utilitarian, using whatever was at hand and the maker's limited expertise and imagination to put together a serviceable object for some household use and purpose.

Roughly hewn as they may have been, some of these pieces do have remarkable integrity. And, because by now they have become quite rare finds, their value has increased dramatically; in fact, rustic pieces of great originality may outstrip in price the professional furniture-maker's highly finished product of a similar age. A hand-

OPPOSITE

Behind the glass doors of this large dresser, a wonderful collection of old china dinner services and tea and coffee sets have been kept safe from family mishap for a remarkable period.

RIGHT

A Georgian mahogany bow-front chest of drawers, circa 1790, may have been an early import, coming to the colony with an affluent free settler.

The finely grained wood and ornate drawer pulls define this sturdy piece as an obvious European import. But by now it's throughly assimilated into our country scene.

This Swedish pine bedroom cupboard, used as a night stand, has a practical marble top for everyday use, yet still looks very decorative.

This authentic old kerosene-tin chest of drawers is a rare and wonderful find. But if you feel inclined to copy the idea, it shouldn't be hard to do.

adzed meat-safe with precisely joined lattice doors may have the refined dimensions of a much more sophisticated piece and these days would probably take pride of place in a living room, housing stereo equipment, storing wine, or hiding the television set.

Ingenuity played a large part in the making of these one-off pieces. Some, of course, were strangely shaped indeed, but it is the integrity of an object which is its real hallmark and not its pedigree or cost that counts. So these improvised products of the bush carpenter's hand took many forms, to make use of whatever could be recycled and used in some new way. Wooden boxes and empty kerosene tins were among the most often rehabilitated into new and functional things. Classic among them were the kerosene-tin chest of drawers and the packing-case cupboard, of so many uses.

More refined pieces were, of course made for wealthier folk. Cabinet-makers from England set up shop to work here, and though conditions may not always have been

A dressing-table with a white marble shelf sports a silver toilet set. Note how the two chairs have been treated: one is elegantly caned; the other, in more countryfied mode, has a rush seat rather too coarse for its style.

RIGHT
A prime example of a Victorian cedar dressing-table displays an antique ivory dressing-table set.

OPPOSITE
This more ornate dressing-table with acorn and oakleaf motif is of European origin. The carved, antique ivory clothes brush is particularly distinctive.

THE REAL STUFF

The pine chair and chiffonier blend well with an old Kelim rug. The footstool is a milking stool.

An English pub chair made of elm marries well with the Huon pine primitive table and is set off by the grey and pink of the Persian rug.

easy or at least as professionally satisfying in the new colony, they made the most of local timbers and often compensated for what was lacking by their use of innovative detail and simplified forms. Fine Australian cedar trees quickly became scarce because their wood had been used enthusiastically in the production of furniture and for architectural joinery. But pine and other timbers played a central role for a very long time.

In due course, trade blossomed in the new colonies, imports arrived by the shipload, and new settlers brought things with them to set up home; as a result, all kinds of homewares took their place in the growing settlements. Even though all this happened over decades rather than centuries, the real stuff we admire today will have surprising diversity, from the roughly hewn and twig furniture to elegant Georgian pieces. The only criterion necessary to apply in judging these things is to assess their integrity. It isn't too difficult to see what is or isn't the real stuff, for it has an ineffable quality of its own.

The muted colour of natural, faded vegetable dyes marks this rug as an authentic old oriental example of pre-aniline-dyes vintage.

A bowl of quinces picked in the kitchen garden rests on a rush-seated chair, perhaps in transit to be made into quince jelly in a pot on the wood-burning stove.

An old wooden chair with quite intricate uprights has a pierced seat, though it and the circular back rest were obviously once caned and must have been a very pretty sight.

A rustic whatnot with rough-sawn plank shelves has uprights crafted from wooden cotton reels. A delightful instance of making do in creative fashion using simple things.

A very beguiling Victorian cast-iron garden chair has a delightfully ornate decoration of blackberries and blackberry leaves.

'The real stuff we admire today will have surprising diversity, from the roughly hewn and twig furniture to elegant Georgian pieces'

A rustic garden seat, soon to be surrounded by the heady perfume of sweet peas in bountiful bloom, adds a restful air to a country garden in Mudgee, New South Wales.

A dilapidated old wicker chair sits on the small veranda of a slab hut as they both pass into peaceful desuetude.

This remarkable old stick chair had an important role to play in households where young children or invalids might need a night commode.

THE REAL STUFF

249

SOURCES

THIS list is not a complete catalogue of places dealing in country furniture and accessories, but it should help you make a start on your country collecting. It's possible that your best buy may be found in some little out-of-the-way place you just discover by chance; in the meantime, you can be sure of finding some wonderful things in the places listed below.

Sources are categorised under certain headings, but no distinction has been made between the up-market antique shops and the stores that specialise in less expensive reproductions.

Familiarising yourself with valuable antiques will give you a better understanding of the character of such objects and their place in history. Whether you're furnishing a tiny cottage or something along the lines of the Trianon, this list should be of help to you.

To the best of our knowledge, the information in this listing is accurate at the time of going to press. Even so, a phone call might be advisable if you are seeking some special item from any particular source.

Country furniture

Andre's Bedsteads
22 Oxford Street
Paddington NSW 2021
Tel. (02) 360 6834

Dealing only in old and genuine fancy lace iron bedsteads. Also restores old brass and iron bedsteads.

The Antique Warehouse
52–56 Mallett Street
Camperdown NSW 2050
Tel. (02) 516 1699

Everything from blanket chests to a wide selection of country chairs can be found under this roof.

Appley Hoare Antiques
5 Queen Street
Woollahra NSW 2025
Tel. (02) 362 3045

European country wares, unique and rare pieces for the dedicated collector but not for bargain hunters.

Australian Squatter's Chair
  Company
54 Spit Road
Mosman NSW 2088
Tel. (02) 968 2291

Cast-iron fireplace tools, boot scrapers, wooden letterboxes and more. Also garden and outdoor furniture

Chelsea House Antique Centre
160 Parramatta Road
Camperdown NSW 2050
Tel. (02) 516 2737

More than fifty-five shops here to make your search easier. Everything from porcelains to pine and cedar furniture.

Colonial Charm
3 Eastlake Street
Carrara Qld 4211
Tel. (075) 30 2884

Recycled timber is used to make these colonial-style hutches, tables, chairs, etc. Special commissions are taken.

Colonial Cottage
105 Hume Highway
Mittagong NSW 2575
Tel. (048) 71 3530

From simple grain scoops to commodious cupboards and chests, there's an amazing variety of country things here.

Copeland & De Soos
66 Queen Street
Woollahra NSW 2025
Tel. (02) 32 5288

While this dealer specialises in twentieth-century decorative arts, you will also find superlative examples of the country genre.

Cottage Kitchen Antiques
278 Barker Road
Subiaco WA 6008
Tel. (09) 381 8818

Antique and reproduction pine furniture, light fittings and brass hardware, as well as damask linen and fine old china.

Country Runner Antiques &
  Restorations
529a King Street
Newtown NSW 2042
Tel. (02) 516 4637

Colonial, Federation and country furniture bought and sold. You could sell or upgrade here.

Country Style Interiors
129 Waratah Avenue
Dalkeith WA 6009
Tel. (09) 386 7195

Country furniture designed in uncomplicated style: large commodious dressers, rush-seated chairs and tablewares.

Country Form
1152 High Street
Armadale Vic. 3143
Tel. (03) 500 9664

Hand-crafted furniture with more than a hint of European country chic. Two stylish stores in Sydney as well.

Country Furniture Antiques
402 Darling Street
Balmain NSW 2041
Tel. (02) 810 8446

Nineteenth-century pine and country furniture, sparingly renovated and authentically presented. European and local pieces.

Country Workshop Antiques
11 Station Street
Malvern Vic. 4144
Tel. (03) 509 9426

From ironware candelabra to wooden cutlery trays, from corner cupboards to commodious kitchen tables.

Flossoms
11 Military Road
Neutral Bay NSW 2089
Tel. (02) 953 7766

Original Australian antiques, period pieces and reproductions in an enticing warehouse-sized showroom.

For Love of Country
85 Queen Street
Berry NSW 2535
Tel. (044) 64 1648

This is a specialists' heaven with a most exciting collection of authentic country furniture and accessories, all well aged.

Furniture in the Raw
378 Pacific Highway
Crows Nest NSW 2065
Tel. (02) 439 8635

Sturdy, simple furniture in solid timbers like blackwood, Tasmanian oak and pine, many crafted to suit country style.

Grange Galerie
422 Military Road
Cremorne NSW 2090
Tel. (02) 953 9277

Beautifully crafted cane tables and comfortable chairs. Reproduction Shaker chests of drawers and much, much more.

Harmony Antiques
128 George Street
East Fremantle WA 6158
Tel. (09) 339 6789

Authentic country furniture, not only Australian, but European pieces as well, for collectors of the unusual.

J & H Furniture
1 Fielding Way
Ulverstone Tas. 7315
Tel. (004) 25 3281

Handmade reproductions, in blackwood, myrtle and Huon pine, of Georgian and Regency pieces, and antiques as well.

Kiama Antique Centre
42 Terralong Street
Kiama NSW 2533
Tel. (042) 32 2357

Country crafted furniture, old ceramic pieces and accessories of all kinds to create the country look.

Mountain Style Country
   Furniture & Collectibles
53 Katoomba Street
Katoomba NSW 2780
Tel. (047) 82 5333

Old lining-board cupboards, painted stools and benches, baskets, chairs and old china and textiles.

1901 Furniture Co.
50 Musgrave Road
Red Hill Qld 4059
Tel. (07) 368 2222

Colonial furniture reproduced from designs of the late 1800s; miner's couches, chests of drawers, desks and chairs.

Rosebank Cottage
Cnr Upton and Ashmore Roads
Surfers Paradise Qld 4217
Tel. (075) 38 6206

Hand-crafted furniture made from aged, old timber. Bedside and blanket chests, screens, towel rails and more.

Rustic Charm
637 Military Road
Mosman NSW 2088
Tel. (02) 960 3328

Countryfied antiques and gifts for people and houses. Accessories to put the ideal finish to country style.

The Tin Shed
148 Beattie Street
Balmain NSW 2041
Tel. (02) 555 1042

A quite remarkable collection of rustic, weathered survivors of the country environment.

Village Antiques
Jellore Street
Berrima NSW 2577
Tel. (048) 77 1366

Country furniture of the eighteenth and nineteenth centuries, both Australian and European; half-testers and four-posters.

Country accessories

Berrima Galleries
Hume Highway
Berrima NSW 2577
Tel. (048) 77 1333

All the little extras to create the country look: baskets, bowls, candles, wall hangings and more.

Berry Antiques
83 Queen Street
Berry NSW 2535
Tel. (044) 64 1552

Jam-packed with Australiana and quaint old things of every conceivable kind to add character to country style.

Crowded House Design
62 Glenferrie Road
Malvern Vic. 3144
Tel. (03) 500 0328

Painted and plain wooden furniture as well as decorative accessories of all kinds for the country look.

National Trust Shops, Sydney
Roma Arcade, Double Bay
Tel. (02) 258 0154
Juniper Hall, Oxford Street
Tel. (02) 331 6947
961 Pacific Highway, Pymble
Tel. (02) 44 1780

Delightful accessories of all kinds to establish an easy country atmosphere; Screen-printed cushions filled with flowers and herbs, tea towels, bookmarks and books with Australian style.

Janet Niven
118 Queen Street
Woollahra NSW 2025
Tel. (02) 32 2211

Antique collectibles, miniatures and samplers, porcelain and silver, Georgian and country furniture.

Tim McCormick
53 Queen Street
Woollahra NSW 2025
Tel. (02) 32 5383

Australiana; colonial paintings; rare books, prints and photographs; fine accessories for the discerning.

Sweet Liberty
163 Princes Highway
Narooma NSW 2546
Tel. (044) 76 1378

Useful hand-painted wooden items, quilts and patchwork fabrics, rag dolls and animals all with a country flavour.

Tony Ward's Printique
94 Queen Street
Woollahra NSW 2025
Tel. (02) 32 1422

Gould's *Birds of Australia*, botanical prints and Australian historical prints and antique maps.

The White Birch
Shop 7, Manuka Village
Manuka ACT 2063
Tel. (062) 95 9609

Hand-worked linen and lace for bedroom or dining room; botanical prints and country-style accessories.

Quilts

Hearts & Hands
351 Great Western Highway
Bullaburra NSW 2784
Tel. (047) 59 2424

Quilts and patchwork, hand- and machine-stitched by thirteen keen quilters. Quilts can also be made to order.

Trish Hurst, interior consultant
(at home by appointment)
60 Holt Avenue
Mosman NSW 2090
Tel. (02) 953 3364

A very beautiful range of antique quilts. Also folk art, whirlygigs and Old Order Amish dolls, all rare.

Keepsake Quilts
6 Avonside Road
Belgrave Heights Vic. 3106
Tel. (03) 754 4189

Hand-crafted quilts from cot size to king-size. Continental quilt covers and pillow shams in many colours and styles.

Patchwork Supplies
43 Gloucester Street
Highgate Hill Qld 4104
Tel. (07) 844 9391

For DIY enthusiasts: books, accessories, quilt patterns, fabrics plain or patterned. Mail orders are welcomed. Classes with expert tutors.

The Quilting Bee
14 The Village Arcade
Pacific Highway
Gordon NSW 2072
Tel. (02) 499 2203

New and antique quilts, or quilts commissioned to special order if you have a particular design in mind.

Bed, bath and table linen

Belinda's Corner Shop
Cnr Ross Street and St John's
   Road
Glebe NSW 2037
Tel. (02) 552 3190

Bed and table linen, Ozzie Mozzie nets, beds and bedroom things, paintings and accessories.

Brett Products
School Street
Balmain East NSW 2041
Tel. (02) 810 0711

Tent and sail makers—a surprise listing, but an excellent source of natural cotton canvas for simple, inexpensive curtaining.

Cast Iron Bath Suppliers Co.
450 Botany Road
Beaconsfield NSW 2015
Tel. (02) 698 4000

For those wanting to recreate an old-fashioned bathroom, antique-style, free-standing footed baths are available.

Dimity's Cottage
61 Burns Bay Road
Lane Cove NSW 2066
Tel. (02) 428 4454

Fabrics and wall coverings;

handmade patchwork and appliquéd quilts.

Lillywhites
Wahroonga Village Stores
62–66 Coonanbarra Road
Wahroonga NSW 2076
Tel. (02) 487 1178

Linen and lace for the authentic country details, as well as silver objects and early Australian pine furniture in fitting style.

Floor coverings and tiles

Bennett's Magill Pottery Pty Ltd
Briant Road
Magill SA 5072
Tel. (08) 31 1340

Tile patterns to restore Federation verandas and bathrooms perfectly, also plain and border tiles.

Robin Cosgrove Rugs
28 Cross Street
Double Bay NSW 2028
Tel. (02) 362 3663

A wonderfully diverse array of rugs designed to the proprietor's order, as well as fascinating old Kelims. Ideal country style.

Country Floors
28 Moncur Street
Woollahra NSW 2025
Tel. (02) 326 2444

Hand-painted and imported tiles, as well as Federation and every other pattern for renovating and renewal.

Designer Rugs
Shop 5, 84 George Street
The Rocks NSW 2000
Tel. (02) 252 3465
In Perth (09) 455 2633

Hand-tufted, custom-made rugs that give you the chance for complete individuality in the choice of a rug for your country-style decorating.

Josephine Kelly
The Ridgeway
Lisarow NSW 2250
Tel. (043) 67 6112

Hand-braided rugs made to special order on commission. Slides of her work can be seen at the Craft Council, 127 George Street, Sydney.

The Natural Floorcovering
  Centre
5 Salisbury Road
Stanmore NSW 2048
Tel. (02) 569 6999

For natural, inexpensive floor coverings, ideal in a country setting; coir and sisal mattings in abundance.

Pazotti
108 Wellington Road
East Brisbane Qld 4169
Tel. (07) 391 8031

Imported terracotta tiles, handpainted feature tiles in modules to suit terrace, bathroom or kitchen

Regeneration
101 Bay Street
Port Melbourne Vic. 3207
Tel. (03) 64 1515

Tiles for every renovation, Federation veranda, wall, floor and accent tiles for bathrooms and kitchens.

Renditions Pty Ltd
112 Pyrmont Bridge Road
Camperdown NSW 2050
Tel. (02) 516 4066

Federation geometric floor tiles for the restoration of hallway, veranda or bathroom, plus many more.

Rogers, Seller & Myhill Pty Ltd
27 City Road
South Melbourne Vic. 3205
Tel. (03) 62 0781

Every conceivable style of tile from the most simple to the most extravagant bathroom de luxe.

Whitecliffe Imports
41 Mallett Street
Camperdown NSW 2050
Tel. (02) 550 2400

This range of imported rugs has something for everyone. Phone them for showrooms in Melbourne, Brisbane, Adelaide.

Woodstock
116 Union Street
Surrey Hills Vic. 3127
Tel. (03) 830 4447

Hand-hooked, 100 per cent wool rugs, hall and stairway runners in colourful designs inspired by Claire Murray's Nantucket.

Garden furniture and furnishings

Colonial Hardware Co.
180 Latrobe Terrace
Paddington Qld 4064
Tel. (07) 369 3171

Reproduction garden seats to add authenticity to an old-fashioned garden can be found here.

Cotswold Garden Furniture
61 Boundary Street
Roseville NSW 2069
Tel. (02) 417 4532

Agent for English teak garden furniture. Phone them for stockists nearest you and your garden.

Emerald Hill Gallery
193 Bank Street
South Melbourne Vic. 3205
Tel. (03) 375 3773

For Dickie Blackburn's splendid hand-crafted garden seats (also benches and rush-seated chairs) this, and other outlets.

Gardenesque
14 William Street
South Yarra Vic. 3141
Tel. (03) 241 8526

Old-fashioned garden edging tiles, to keep things neat, can be found here, along with almost everything else you need.

Valerie Lawson
Argyle Street
Moss Vale NSW 2577
Tel. (048) 68 3066

Antiques for the house and wonderfully crafted garden things to set the scene outside.

The Parterre Garden
33 Ocean Street
Woollahra NSW 2025
Tel. (02) 363 5874

A wonderland of terrace, veranda and outdoor things from bronzed candlesticks to teak garden seats: all desirable.

The Rose Arbour
154 Wattle Tree Road
Malvern Vic. 3144
Tel. (03) 500 0251

A wonderful collection of bent-wire plant stands and Victorian garden arches to inspire a cottage gardener.

253

The School of Arts 1891
Argyle Street
Moss Vale NSW 2577
Tel. (048) 68 3066

Antique and garden things from candlesticks to the most elaborate Victorian gazebo in wrought iron.

. . . and Woven Cane
194 Boundary Road
Bardon Qld 4065
Tel. (075) 368 1531

For verandas, patios and terraces, restored old and antique cane pieces. Bentwood too, plus caning material.

Reproductions for restorations

Architectural Heritage
62 Glebe Point Road
Glebe NSW 2037
Tel. (02) 660 0100

Restored chimney pieces, four- and six-panel doors, Victorian and Federation columns and lacework.

Colonial Hardware and
  Lighting Co.
278 Unley Road
Hyde Park SA 5061
Tel. (08) 271 3342

A huge stock of period hardware and lighting. For the dedicated home restorer, it's a find.

Full Circle Architectural
  Antiques
59 Church Street
Hawthorn Vic. 3122
Tel. (03) 818 1474

Everything from feature tiles to fireplace tools; porcelain door plates to pendant room lights.

The House of Fretworks
73 High Street
Prahran Vic. 3181
Tel. (03) 529 5574

For interiors, front entrances, verandas and gables; a choice of red cedar, oregon, pine, or kauri woods for renovation.

Magin's
169 Stirling Highway
Nedlands WA 6009
Tel. (09) 386 6057

A splendid array of the best in household hardware; Victoriana to delight the discerning home restorer.

Mother of Pearl & Sons
574 Willoughby Road
Willoughby NSW 2068
Tel. (02) 958 6355

Hardware in porcelain, brass and wood; door pulls, knobs, hinges and latches—a big stock of renovation items.

Nineteenth Century Door and
  Hardware Co.
Antique Centre, Cordelia Street
South Brisbane Qld 4101
Tel. (07) 44 8514

Finding so much sought-after hardware under one roof will be a boon to the busy home renovator and restorer.

Porta Pty Ltd
224–56 Heidelberg Road
Fairfield Vic. 3078
Tel. (03) 481 6211

For interiors only: doors and door frames. A wide range of mouldings in a variety of imported woods.

The Restoration Centre
276 Devonshire Street
Surry Hills NSW 2010
Tel. (02) 698 5540

Reproduction cast-iron latches, rim locks, door pulls and shutter fasteners and cast-iron curtain brackets.

The Restorers
92 Jarrett Street
Leichhardt NSW 2040
Tel. (02) 427 7121

For repair and renovation: upholstery and leathering as well as cabinet-making. A very useful service.

Wooden venetian blinds and lattice

Ashdown Blinds Pty Ltd
21–23 Gerald Street
Marrickville NSW 2204
Tel. (02) 519 5329

Cedar wood blinds come in various slat widths. Will restore or repaint most timber blinds.

Campbell & Johnson Pty Ltd
139 Lonsdale Street
Melbourne Vic. 3000
Tel. (03) 663 2649

Timber venetian blinds have done sterling service in country houses as the simplest climate control.

The House of Lattice
314 Bronte Road
Waverley NSW 2024
Tel. (02) 387 8922

Lattice can give a whole new look to gates, fence panels and breezeways and can be custom made to measure.

John Thurlow & Sons Pty Ltd
31 Frodsham Street
Albion Qld 4010
Tel. (07) 262 2444

Timber venetian blinds for both external and inside installation, the ideal things for shade.

The Timber Trellis Company
96 Albion Street
Surry Hills NSW 2010
Tel. (02) 212 4428

For veranda screens, fence and pergola panels, lattice gives the perfect blend of sunshine and shade.

Information and accommodation

The Australian Garden History Society
PO Box 300
Edgecliff NSW 2027

Write for information on old gardens and plantings if you're planning one of your own.

The Resource Centre
Historic Houses Trust
Lyndhurst
61 Darghan Street
Glebe NSW 2037

This centre has been set up to assist dedicated owners of old houses who want advice on authentic restoration detail.

Elizabeth Farm
70 Alice Street
Harris Park NSW 2142
Tel. (02) 635 9488

Elizabeth Farm is open to the public and worthy of your visit. Phone for details of opening hours.

Lanyon
ACT Parks and Conservation Service
Tel. (062) 95 5111

Definitely should be on the agenda if you're visiting Canberra. Call this number for address and opening time.

Wollombi House
Wollombi NSW 2325
For reservations
Tel. (049) 98 3316

This small guest house can take four adults (with camp beds for family use), and children are always welcome.

Further reading

APPERLEY, RICHARD; IRVING, ROBERT; and REYNOLDS, PETER. *A Pictorial Guide to Identifying Australian Architecture*. Angus & Robertson, Sydney, 1989.

BELL, PETER. *Timber and Tin*. University of Queensland Press, St Lucia, Qld, 1984.

BROADBENT, JAMES; EVANS, IAN; and LUCAS, CLIVE. *The Golden Decade of Australian Architecture*. David Ell Press, Sydney, 1978.

CANTLON, MAURICE. *The Homesteads of Southern New South Wales 1830–1900*. Queensberry Hill Press, Carlton, Vic., 1981.

———. *Homesteads of Victoria 1836–1900*. Georgian House, Melbourne, 1967.

CRAIG, C.; FAHY, K.; and ROBERTSON, E.G. *Early Colonial Furniture in New South Wales and Van Diemen's Land*. Georgian House, Melbourne, 1985.

COX, PHILIP, and LUCAS, CLIVE. *Australian Colonial Architecture*. Lansdowne Editions, East Melbourne, 1978.

EVANS, IAN. *The Australian House*. Flannel Flower Press, Sydney, 1983.

———. *The Australian Old House Catalogue*. Methuen Haynes, Sydney, 1984.

FORGE, SUZANNE. *Victorian Splendour*. Oxford University Press, Melbourne, 1981.

FREEMAN, PETER. *The Homestead: A Riverina Anthology*. Oxford University Press, Melbourne, 1982.

GRIFFITHS, G. NESTA. *Some Northern Homes of New South Wales*. Ure Smith, Sydney, 1954.

———. *Some Southern Homes of New South Wales*. Ure Smith, Sydney, 1952.

The Heritage of Australia. Macmillan, 1981.

HERMAN, MORTON. *The Early Australian Architects and Their Work*. Angus & Robertson, Sydney, 1954.

HILL, ANTHONY. *Antique Furniture in Australia*. Viking, Melbourne, 1985.

Historic Homesteads of Australia, vol. 1. Cassell, Melbourne, 1969.

Historic Homesteads of Australia, vol. 2. Cassell, Sydney, 1976.

IRVING, ROBERT (comp.). *The History and Design of the Australian House*. Oxford University Press, Melbourne, 1985.

KERR, JOAN, and BROADBENT, JAMES. *Gothick Taste in the Colony of New South Wales*. David Ell Press, Sydney, 1980.

LUCAS, CLIVE, and JOYCE, RAY. *Australian Country Houses*. Lansdowne Press, Sydney, 1987.

ROBERTSON, E. GRAEME. *Adelaide Lace*. Rigby, Adelaide, 1973.

SIMPSON, CAROLINE, et al. *Australian Antiques: First Fleet to Federation*. Golden Press in association with the National Trust of Australia (NSW), Sydney, 1977.

TANNER, HOWARD (ed.). *Architects of Australia*. Macmillan, Melbourne, 1981.

TAYLOR, PETER. *An Australian Country Life*. Allen & Unwin, Sydney, 1986.

WATTS, PETER. *Historic Gardens of Victoria*. Oxford University Press, Melbourne, 1983.